The True Mediterranean Diet Cookbook for Beginners:

140 Bold and Tasty Recipes for Lifelong Health and Vibrant Living (Includes 35-Day Meal Plan for Easy, Delicious Meals Every Day)

Exclusive Bonus - 50 Additional Mediterranean Recipes eBook

Oliver Maxwell

Legal Notice

The publisher and author have made every effort to ensure that the recipes and related information in this book are accurate and adhere to generally accepted culinary standards at the time of publication. However, the publisher and author do not warrant that the recipe ingredients or instructions contained herein will always achieve the desired result. The effectiveness of recipes may vary based on the quality of ingredients, cooking equipment, or environmental factors. It is the reader's responsibility to determine the value and quality of any recipe or instructions provided for food preparation and to ensure that the food is prepared safely.

Disclaimer Notice

This cookbook is intended for informational purposes only and is not a substitute for professional dietary advice or services. While the recipes in the "Mediterranean Diet Cookbook for Beginners" are designed to promote a healthier lifestyle through the principles of the Mediterranean diet, they should not be considered a substitute for professional medical advice. Always seek the advice of a qualified healthcare provider with any questions you may have regarding a medical condition or dietary needs. The author and publisher expressly disclaim any liability for any adverse effects resulting from the use of the suggestions or information contained herein. Furthermore, the recipes in this book may not be suitable for all individuals, particularly those with specific dietary restrictions or health conditions. Always consult with a healthcare professional before starting any new diet, especially if you have any health-related concerns.

Table of Contents

INTRODUCTION

Welcome to the Mediterranean Diet Cookbook! This book is your passport to a way of life centered around delicious, wholesome meals influenced by the cooking customs of Mediterranean-bordering nations. The Mediterranean diet is renowned for its health advantages and emphasis on whole, natural foods. It can be found anywhere from the sun-drenched coasts of Greece and Italy to the bustling marketplaces of Morocco and Spain.

The Mediterranean diet is a way of life, not just a method of eating. It emphasizes fresh fruit and vegetables, whole grains, lean meats, and healthy fats—especially olive oil. This diet minimizes the intake of processed foods and red meat while promoting moderate consumption of dairy and alcohol. The result is a healthy, balanced diet associated with several health advantages, such as a lower risk of heart disease, stroke, and some types of cancer.

This cookbook offers a selection of dishes that are flavorful and nutrient-dense, in addition to being simple to make. Every meal is created to emphasize the essential elements of the Mediterranean diet so you can fully benefit from all of its health advantages while appreciating each delicious bite. This book has plenty of options to suit every palate and occasion, whether you are new to the Mediterranean diet or want to try more recipes.

Eating Mediterranean-style involves more than just what's on your plate. It's also about relishing food flavors, spending time with loved ones, and appreciating the preparation and sharing of meals. This cookbook encourages you to take it leisurely and enjoy the basic pleasures of cooking and eating.

As you delve into the recipes in this book, you'll encounter a diverse range of dishes that showcase the rich culinary legacy of the Mediterranean region. The recipes, which range from filling feasts and sweet treats to robust breakfasts and light lunches, are designed to bring the colorful tastes of the Mediterranean into your kitchen.

We sincerely hope this cookbook will encourage you to adopt a Mediterranean diet. Cheers to a tasty and well-being trip across the Mediterranean!

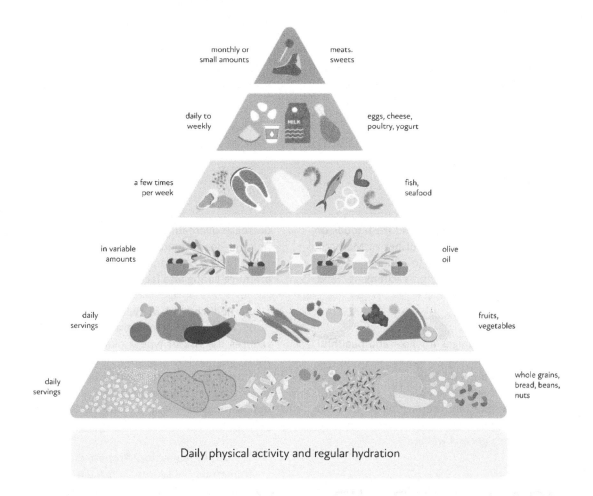

What is the Mediterranean Diet? Why Choose the Mediterranean Diet?

The historic eating habits of nations bordering the Mediterranean Sea, such as Greece, Italy, Spain, and southern France, inspire the Mediterranean diet. This diet promotes a balanced, wholesome, and pleasurable approach to eating while emphasizing whole, natural foods. It's more than just a diet; it's a way of life associated with several long-term health advantages.

Essential Elements of a Mediterranean Diet: Fruits and Veggies Fresh fruits and vegetables, which are high in vitamins, minerals, and antioxidants, are a staple of the Mediterranean diet. The diet is focused mainly on these plant-based foods, focusing on locally and seasonally available produce.

The tasty, healthful cuisine and fantastic health advantages of the Mediterranean diet have made it famous worldwide. However, what distinguishes this eating pattern from other dietary strategies? The following are solid arguments for you to think about implementing a Mediterranean diet:

1. Proven Health Benefits

Numerous studies have emphasized the health benefits of the Mediterranean diet. It has been linked to a lower risk of stroke, heart disease, and several cancers. The diet's focus on heart-healthy fats, such as those in nuts and olive oil, lowers bad cholesterol while raising good cholesterol. A high fruit, vegetable, and whole grain intake also supplies vital vitamins, minerals, and antioxidants that promote general health.

2. Weight Management

Nutrient-dense foods make you feel full and satisfied and help you resist the urge to overeat. This is why the Mediterranean diet promotes the eating of these foods. Incorporating foods high in fiber, lean proteins, and healthy fats encourages fullness and aids in maintaining a healthy weight. In contrast to restrictive diets, the Mediterranean diet provides a long-term, gratifying, and sustainable way of eating.

3. Balanced Nutrition

The Mediterranean diet is naturally balanced and includes a wide range of food groups. Fresh fruits and vegetables, along with whole grains, legumes, nuts, seeds, fish, and modest amounts of chicken and dairy products, are abundant. This varied consumption guarantees that you receive a wide range of nutrients, encouraging optimum health and lowering the possibility of nutrient deficits.

4. Simplicity and Flexibility

The Mediterranean diet's biggest benefits are its flexibility and ease of use. It doesn't call for intricate regulations or rigid food regimens. Rather, it promotes thoughtful eating and a focus on complete, natural foods. The fundamentals of the Mediterranean diet are easily customizable to individual tastes, making it a useful and pleasurable eating style.

5. Cultural and Culinary Richness

The cuisines of the Mediterranean region, which are recognized for their rich and varied cuisines, are fundamental to the Mediterranean diet. The Mediterranean diet offers diverse culinary experiences, from the lively and fresh foods of Greece and Italy to the spicy and aromatic dishes of Morocco and Spain. Adopting this diet allows you to experiment with flavors and cooking methods, adding excitement and enjoyment to your meals.

6. Promotes a Healthy Lifestyle

The Mediterranean diet encourages a whole and healthful lifestyle in addition to specific dietary choices. It promotes social interactions, careful eating, and frequent exercise. The Mediterranean way of life is characterized by eating meals with loved ones, relishing each bite, and setting aside time to appreciate the meal. This methodology cultivates a constructive rapport with food and bolsters general welfare.

7. Sustainability

The Mediterranean diet is environmentally sustainable. It strongly emphasizes plant-based diets, which lessen the meat industry's carbon footprint. Selecting seasonal and locally grown foods will help you cut down on food waste and promote sustainable farming methods. Changing to a Mediterranean diet is good for the environment and your health.

Selecting a Mediterranean diet is a wise choice that promotes good health, a balanced way of life, and exciting new gastronomic experiences. The Mediterranean diet offers a complete and pleasurable way to eat, regardless of your goals: weight management, culinary exploration, or overall health improvement. Accept this traditional eating pattern and reap its numerous benefits.

Health Benefits

One of the world's healthiest dietary regimens is generally considered the Mediterranean diet. It is a well-liked option for people looking to enhance their general well-being because of its emphasis on whole, natural foods and balanced nutrition, which has been connected to several health advantages. The following are some of the most important health advantages of the Mediterranean diet:

1. Heart Health

The heart-protective benefits of the Mediterranean diet are well known. It can considerably lower the risk of cardiovascular disorders, such as heart attacks and strokes, according to numerous research. The high concentration of omega-3 fatty acids from fish and monounsaturated fats from olive oil helps raise good cholesterol (HDL) levels and decrease bad cholesterol (LDL) levels. Furthermore, the diet's emphasis on whole grains, nuts, fruits, and vegetables delivers vital minerals and antioxidants that promote heart health.

2. Weight Management

The Mediterranean diet can help prevent obesity and control weight. To help create a sensation of fullness and decrease overeating, the diet encourages the consumption of nutrient-dense foods that are naturally low in calories and fiber. The Mediterranean lifestyle's emphasis on exercise and attentive eating also facilitates maintaining a healthy weight.

3. Reduced Risk of Type 2 Diabetes

It has been demonstrated that a Mediterranean diet reduces the risk of type 2 diabetes. Its high fiber intake from fruits, vegetables, and whole grains helps to increase insulin sensitivity and control blood sugar levels. The low-glycemic index foods in the diet help reduce blood sugar, so it's a good option for people who already have diabetes or are at risk of getting it.

4. Anti-Inflammatory Properties

Numerous diseases, including cancer, autoimmune disorders, and heart disease, are significantly influenced by chronic inflammation. Anti-inflammatory foods like fruits, vegetables, nuts, seeds, and olive oil are abundant in the Mediterranean diet and can help lower inflammation. Another critical factor in the diet's ability to reduce inflammation is the high concentration of phytochemicals and antioxidants in plant based meals.

5. Improved Brain Health

The Mediterranean diet enhances cognitive abilities and overall brain health. Studies have indicated that it may lower the risk of neurological illnesses, including Parkinson's and Alzheimer's. The diet's high consumption of omega-3 fatty acids from fish and antioxidants from fruits and vegetables promotes brain health by reducing oxidative stress and inflammation.

6. Longevity

Following a Mediterranean diet has been linked to longer life expectancy. Like those in the Mediterranean region, people who consume this way typically live longer and are in better condition. They also tend to have lower rates of chronic diseases. The diet's emphasis on a balanced, healthy intake, an active lifestyle, and solid social relationships enhances overall well-being and lifespan.

7. Digestive Health

The Mediterranean diet benefits digestive health because fruits, vegetables, legumes, and whole grains provide a high fiber level. Fiber facilitates regular bowel movements and keeps constipation at bay, which helps with digestion. Furthermore, eating foods that have undergone fermentation, like kefir and yogurt, gives you good bacteria that help maintain a balanced gut flora.

8. Bone Health

The Mediterranean diet can prevent osteoporosis and support bone health. Dairy products like cheese and yogurt contain calcium necessary for strong bones. Consuming leafy greens, nuts, and seeds also helps maintain healthy bones since they include essential nutrients like vitamin K and magnesium.

The Mediterranean diet is a lifestyle that provides a comprehensive approach to health and well-being, not just a method of eating. When you adopt the Mediterranean diet's tenets into your everyday routine, you can experience the many health advantages of this tried-and-true eating pattern, along with a wide range of delectable meals.

How to Use This Book

Welcome to the Mediterranean Diet Cookbook! This book is designed to guide you through the delicious and nutritious world of Mediterranean cuisine, offering a variety of recipes that are easy to prepare and packed with health benefits. Here's how to make the most of this cookbook:

1. Getting Started

Before diving into the recipes, take a moment to read the introductory sections of the book. These chapters provide valuable information about the Mediterranean diet, its history, and its associated health benefits. Understanding the principles and philosophy behind this diet will help you appreciate the recipes and make informed choices about your meals.

2. Navigating the Recipes

The recipes in this cookbook are organized into several categories to make finding what you're looking for easy. Each section focuses on different types of meals, including breakfasts, lunches, dinners, snacks, and desserts. Use the table of contents to quickly locate the category or specific recipe you want to try.

3. Understanding the Recipe Format

Each recipe is presented with a consistent format that includes the following elements:

Recipe Name: The title of the dish.
Yield: The number of servings the recipe makes.
Prep Time: The estimated time needed to prepare the ingredients.

Cook Time: The estimated time required to cook the dish.
Ingredients: This is a list of all the ingredients you will need, with measurements specified in imperial units to suit the US market. *Directions*: Step-by-step instructions to guide you through the preparation and cooking process.
Nutritional Information: Key nutritional details per serving, including calories, protein, carbohydrates, fat, fiber, cholesterol, sodium, and potassium.

4. Ingredient Substitutions and Variations

Even though the recipes are meant to be simple, you might occasionally need to alter them to suit your dietary needs or the ingredients you already have. Please use your imagination to modify the recipes to your preferences. The Mediterranean diet is adaptable and can take many different forms and substitutes.

5. Meal Planning and Preparation

Consider planning your meals to make your Mediterranean diet journey smooth and enjoyable. Use this cookbook to create weekly meal plans that incorporate a variety of recipes from different categories. Preparing some ingredients, such as chopping vegetables or cooking grains, can save time during busy weekdays and make it easier to stick to your healthy eating goals.

6. Cooking Techniques and Tips

Throughout the book, you will find tips and techniques to enhance your cooking experience. These include advice on selecting the freshest ingredients, proper cooking methods, and ways to maximize the flavors of your dishes. Pay attention to these tips to improve your culinary skills and achieve the best results.

7. Enjoying the Mediterranean Lifestyle

The Mediterranean diet emphasizes cooking and eating, sharing meals with loved ones and friends, and taking pleasure in every bite. Use this cookbook as a resource to adopt a totally Mediterranean diet. To fully benefit from this healthy style of living, try combining social contacts, mindfulness, and physical activity into your everyday routine.

8. Expanding Your Repertoire

As you become more comfortable with the recipes and cooking techniques, challenge yourself to try new dishes and experiment with different flavors. The Mediterranean diet offers a rich culinary heritage with endless possibilities. Keep exploring and expanding your repertoire to keep your meals exciting and enjoyable.

This cookbook is your comprehensive guide to embracing the Mediterranean diet and all its wonderful flavors and health benefits. Whether you are new to this way of eating or looking to deepen your culinary skills, this book provides the tools and inspiration to make delicious, nutritious meals a regular part of your life. Happy cooking!

Kitchen Equipment

Having the right kitchen equipment is essential to embrace and enjoy the Mediterranean diet fully. The following tools and appliances will help you easily prepare various delicious and nutritious dishes.

Essential Kitchen Equipment

1. Chef's Knife
A high-quality chef's knife is a must-have for any kitchen. It is versatile and can be used for chopping, slicing, dicing, and mincing various ingredients, from vegetables to meats.

2. Cutting Board
Invest in a sturdy wood or plastic cutting board. Having multiple boards for different types of food (e.g., one for vegetables and another for meats) can help prevent cross-contamination.

3. Mixing Bowls
A set of mixing bowls in various sizes is essential for preparing and mixing ingredients. Stainless steel, glass, or ceramic bowls are durable and easy to clean.

4. Measuring Cups and Spoons
Accurate measurements are crucial for the success of many recipes. A set of measuring cups and spoons will ensure you use each ingredient correctly.

5. Saucepan
A medium-sized saucepan is perfect for cooking grains, making sauces, and simmering soups. Choose a saucepan with a heavy bottom to prevent scorching.

6. Skillet
A good-quality skillet, preferably non-stick or cast iron, is essential for sautéing vegetables, searing meats, and cooking various dishes.

7. Baking Sheet
A baking sheet is versatile. It can be used for roasting vegetables, baking fish, or making cookies. Look for one with a non-stick surface, or use parchment paper to prevent sticking.

8. Blender or Food Processor
A blender or food processor is invaluable for making smoothies, sauces, dips, and dressings. It can also be used to chop nuts and puree soups.

9. Salad Spinner

A salad spinner is essential for washing and drying leafy greens. Dry greens are more accessible to dress and less likely to wilt.

10. Garlic Press

A garlic press makes mincing garlic quick and easy, ensuring even flavor distribution in your dishes.

11. Grater or Microplane

A grater or microplane grates cheese, zesting citrus fruits, and shredding vegetables.

12. Colander

A colander is necessary for draining pasta, washing vegetables, and rinsing canned beans. Choose one with sturdy handles and a stable base.

13. Tongs

Tongs are versatile tools for flipping, tossing, and serving food. Look for tongs with a good grip and a locking mechanism for easy storage.

14. Whisk

A whisk is essential for blending ingredients smoothly, whether making vinaigrettes, beating eggs, or mixing batters.

15. Ovenproof Dish

An ovenproof dish, such as a casserole dish or a Dutch oven, is ideal for baking and roasting. It can go from stovetop to oven, making it versatile for various recipes.

Additional Useful Tools

1. Mandoline

A mandoline slicer is perfect for creating uniformly thin slices of vegetables, enhancing the presentation and cooking of your dishes.

2. Mortar and Pestle

A mortar and pestle are traditional tools for grinding spices, making pesto, and creating other pastes and spreads.

3. Citrus Juicer

A citrus juicer makes extracting fresh juice from lemons, limes, and oranges easy. It is often used in Mediterranean recipes.

4. Immersion Blender

An immersion blender is handy for pureeing soups directly in the pot and making quick sauces and smoothies.

5. Kitchen Scale

A kitchen scale ensures precise measurement of ingredients by weight, which can be especially important for baking.

6. Peeler

A vegetable peeler is useful for peeling fruits and vegetables quickly and efficiently.

Equipping your kitchen with these essential tools and appliances will make preparing Mediterranean dishes more enjoyable and efficient. With the right equipment, you can confidently explore the rich culinary traditions of the Mediterranean and create healthy, delicious meals for yourself and your family.

Basic Cooking Techniques

Mastering basic cooking techniques is essential for preparing delicious and nutritious Mediterranean dishes. These techniques will help you bring out the best flavors and textures in your ingredients, ensuring that your meals are satisfying and healthy. Here are some fundamental cooking techniques used in Mediterranean cuisine:

1. Sautéing

Sautéing involves cooking food quickly in a small amount of oil over medium to high heat. This method is ideal for vegetables, seafood, and thin cuts of meat. To sauté:

- Heat a small amount of olive oil in a skillet over medium-high heat.
- Add the food in a single layer, ensuring the pan is not overcrowded.
- Stir or toss the food frequently to ensure even cooking.
- Cook until the food is tender and lightly browned.

2. Roasting

Roasting enhances the natural flavors of vegetables, meats, and fish by cooking them in the oven with dry heat. This technique is excellent for creating caramelized exteriors and tender interiors. To roast:

- Preheat your oven to the desired temperature (usually between 375°F and 425°F).
- Toss the ingredients with olive oil, salt, and pepper.
- Spread the ingredients in a single layer on a baking sheet or roasting pan.
- Roast, stirring occasionally, until the food is golden brown and cooked through.

3. Grilling

Grilling imparts a smoky flavor to food and is perfect for meats, fish, and vegetables. Whether using an outdoor grill or an indoor grill pan, grilling is popular in Mediterranean cooking. To grill:

- Preheat the grill to medium-high heat.
- Brush the food with olive oil and season with salt and pepper.

- Place the food on the grill and cook, turning occasionally, until it is nicely charred and cooked to your desired doneness.

4. Baking

Baking is a versatile cooking method for preparing bread, pastries, casseroles, and more. Baking uses dry heat in an oven to cook food evenly. To bake:
- Preheat your oven to the required temperature.
- Prepare the ingredients according to the recipe.
- Place the food in a baking dish or on a baking sheet.
- Bake until the food is cooked and has reached the desired level of doneness.

5. Boiling

Boiling is a quick and simple method for cooking pasta, grains, and vegetables. To boil:
- Fill a large pot with water and bring it to a rolling boil.
- Add a generous amount of salt to the water.
- Add the food to the boiling water and cook until it reaches the desired texture.
- Drain the food in a colander and rinse with cold water if necessary.

6. Steaming

Steaming is a gentle cooking method that preserves the nutrients and flavor of vegetables, fish, and other delicate foods. To steam:

- Fill a pot with a few inches of water and bring it to a simmer.
- Place a steamer basket over the pot, ensuring the water does not touch the food.
- Add the food to the steamer basket, cover, and cook until tender.

7. Simmering

Simmering involves cooking food in liquid at a temperature just below boiling. This method is ideal for soups, stews, and sauces. To simmer:
- Bring the liquid to a boil in a pot.
- Reduce the heat to low so that tiny bubbles form around the edges of the pot.
- Add the food and cook gently, stirring occasionally, until the flavors are well blended and the food is tender.

8. Blending and Pureeing

Blending and pureeing are techniques used to create smooth soups, sauces, and dips. To blend or puree:
- Place the cooked ingredients in a blender or food processor.
- Blend until the mixture is smooth and creamy.
- Adjust the consistency with additional liquid if necessary.

How to Choose Quality Ingredients

Choosing high-quality ingredients is crucial for creating delicious and nutritious Mediterranean dishes. The Mediterranean diet emphasizes fresh, whole foods, and selecting the best ingredients will elevate your cooking and ensure you get the most health benefits from your meals. Here are some tips on how to choose quality ingredients for your Mediterranean recipes:

1. Fresh Produce

Fruits and Vegetables
Seasonal: Choose fruits and vegetables that are in season. They are usually fresher, tastier, and more affordable.
Local: Whenever possible, buy locally grown produce. It often has a shorter time from farm to table, ensuring better freshness.
Organic: Consider organic options to avoid pesticides and chemicals.
Look and Feel: Select produce that is vibrant in color and free from blemishes. They should feel firm, not too hard or too soft.

2. Olive Oil

Extra-Virgin Olive Oil
Cold-Pressed: Choose extra-virgin olive oil that is cold-pressed to ensure it retains its nutrients and flavor.
Dark Bottle: Opt for olive oil in dark bottles, which protect it from light and preserve its quality.
Freshness: Check the harvest date on the label and choose the freshest oil available. Olive oil is best used within 12 to 18 months of harvest.

3. Fish and Seafood

Fresh and Sustainable
Smell: Fresh fish should have a clean, sea-like smell. Avoid fish with a strong, fishy odor.
Eyes and Gills: Look for clear, bright eyes and vibrant red gills.
Firmness: The flesh should be firm and spring back when touched.
Sustainability: To support ocean health, choose sustainable seafood options. Look for certifications like MSC (Marine Stewardship Council).

4. Meat and Poultry

Lean and Organic

Color: Fresh meat should have a bright color. For beef, look for a deep red; for chicken, a pale pink.

Marbling: For beef, some marbling (fat within the muscle) indicates flavor and tenderness.

Organic and Free-Range: Whenever possible, choose organic and free-range options. They are often higher in nutrients and free from antibiotics and hormones.

5. Dairy Products

Quality and Freshness

Cheese: Choose cheeses made from whole, natural ingredients. Opt for varieties like feta, ricotta, and Parmesan.

Yogurt: Look for plain, unsweetened yogurt with live and active cultures. Greek yogurt is an excellent choice for its high protein content.

Milk: Opt for organic milk to avoid hormones and antibiotics.

6. Grains and Legumes

Whole and Unprocessed

Whole Grains: Choose whole grains like quinoa, bulgur, farro, and whole wheat pasta. They are higher in fiber and nutrients than refined grains.

Legumes: Look for dried or low-sodium canned beans and lentils. They are excellent sources of protein and fiber.

7. Nuts and Seeds

Raw and Unsalted

Freshness: Buy nuts and seeds in small quantities to ensure freshness. Store them in airtight containers in a cool, dark place.

Raw and Unsalted: Choose raw, unsalted nuts and seeds to avoid added sodium and unhealthy fats.

8. Herbs and Spices

Fresh and Fragrant

Fresh Herbs: Whenever possible, use fresh herbs like basil, parsley, cilantro, and mint. They add vibrant flavor and aroma to dishes.

Spices: Choose whole spices and grind them yourself for the best flavor. Store spices in airtight containers away from light and heat.

By selecting high-quality ingredients, you are setting the foundation for delicious and healthful Mediterranean meals. Remember, the key to the Mediterranean diet is freshness and simplicity. Use these tips to choose the best ingredients, and you'll enjoy the full flavors and nutritional benefits of this wholesome way of eating. Happy cooking!

Shopping at Markets and Stores

Shopping for ingredients in markets and stores can be a delightful experience, especially when looking for the freshest and highest quality items to create Mediterranean dishes. Here are some tips and strategies to help you maximize your shopping trips and find the best recipe ingredients.

1. Plan Ahead

Make a List

Before heading out, plan your weekly meals and make a shopping list. This will help you stay focused and ensure you get everything you need.

Know Your Stores

Familiarize yourself with different stores and markets in your area. Specialty stores, farmers' markets, and ethnic markets can offer unique ingredients that may not be available in larger grocery stores.

2. Farmers' Markets

Shop Seasonally

Farmers' markets are the best places to find fresh, seasonal produce. Seasonal fruits and vegetables are usually at their peak in flavor and nutrition.

Talk to Farmers

Engage with farmers and vendors. They can provide valuable insights into how their produce is grown and suggest the best ways to prepare it.

Sample and Choose

Many farmers' markets offer samples. Take advantage of this to taste before you buy, ensuring you get the best quality.

3. Supermarkets

Perimeter Shopping

Focus on the store's perimeter, where fresh produce, dairy, meat, and seafood are located. These areas typically have the freshest and least processed foods.

Check Labels

Read labels carefully, especially when buying packaged foods. Look for items with minimal ingredients and avoid those with additives, preservatives, and artificial flavors.

Organic Options

Choose organic produce, dairy, and meat to avoid pesticides, hormones, and antibiotics when possible.

4. Specialty and Ethnic Markets

Explore New Flavors
Specialty and ethnic markets can be treasure troves of unique ingredients, such as spices, grains, and oils, essential to Mediterranean cuisine.

Buy in Bulk
Many specialty stores offer bulk sections for grains, nuts, and spices. Buying in bulk can be cost-effective and allows you to get precisely the amount you need.

Ask for Advice
Don't hesitate to ask store employees for recommendations on new ingredients and how to use them.

5. Online Shopping

Convenience
Online shopping can be a convenient way to get specialty items that are hard to find locally. Many online retailers offer high-quality ingredients and deliver them directly to your door.

Subscription Services
Consider subscribing to a service that regularly delivers fresh produce or specialty Mediterranean ingredients.

Read Reviews
When buying online, read customer reviews to ensure the quality of the products you are purchasing.

6. Selecting Fresh Produce

Look and Feel
Choose fruits and vegetables that are vibrant in color and free from blemishes. They should feel firm and have a pleasant smell.

Seasonal Shopping
Buy produce that is in season for the best flavor and value. Seasonal produce is often more affordable and abundant.

7. Buying Meat and Seafood

Freshness Indicators
For seafood, look for clear, bright eyes, vibrant red gills, and a fresh, sea-like smell. Meat should be brightly colored and firm to the touch.

Sustainable Choices
Opt for sustainable seafood and meat from grass-fed, free-range, and antibiotic- and hormone-free animals.

Buy Local
Whenever possible, buy from local butchers and fishmongers who can offer fresher options and more personalized service.

8. Dairy and Eggs

Quality Checks
Choose organic dairy products and eggs free from artificial hormones. Look for eggs labeled as free-range or pasture-raised.

Freshness
Check the sell-by dates on dairy products and eggs to ensure they are fresh.

Shopping for Mediterranean ingredients can be a rewarding experience that connects you to your food sources and enhances your culinary adventures. By following these tips and exploring different markets and stores, you can find the freshest and highest-quality ingredients to create delicious and nutritious Mediterranean dishes. Enjoy discovering new flavors and ingredients that will bring your cooking to life.

Tropical Fruit and Coconut Yogurt Parfait

Yield: 2 servings | **Prep time:** 10 minutes | **Cook time:** 0 minutes

Ingredients:
- 2 cups coconut yogurt
- 1 cup mixed tropical fruits (pineapple, mango, papaya), diced
- 1/2 cup granola
- 2 tablespoons shredded coconut
- 2 tablespoons honey

Directions:
1. In two serving glasses or bowls, add a layer of coconut yogurt (1/2 cup each).
2. Add a layer of mixed tropical fruits (1/4 cup each) on top of the yogurt.
3. Sprinkle a layer of granola (2 tablespoons each) over the fruits.
4. Repeat the layers, ending with a sprinkle of shredded coconut on top.
5. Drizzle 1 tablespoon of honey over each parfait.
6. Serve immediately and enjoy!

Nutritional Information: 320 calories, 5g protein, 50g carbohydrates, 12g fat, 3g fiber, 0mg cholesterol, 80mg sodium, 350mg potassium.

Note: Nutritional values are estimated based on the ingredients and serving size. Actual values may vary slightly. The final presentation of your recipe may vary slightly from the image illustration.

Apple Cinnamon Yogurt Bowl

Yield: 2 servings | **Prep time:** 10 minutes | **Cook time:** 0 minutes

Ingredients:
- 2 cups Greek yogurt
- 1 apple, diced
- 1 teaspoon ground cinnamon
- 2 tablespoons honey
- 1/4 cup granola
- 2 tablespoons chopped walnuts

Directions:
1. In two serving bowls, divide the Greek yogurt evenly (1 cup each).
2. In a small bowl, mix the diced apple with ground cinnamon.
3. Top each bowl of yogurt with half of the cinnamon-coated apple.
4. Drizzle 1 tablespoon of honey over each serving.
5. Sprinkle 2 tablespoons of granola and 1 tablespoon of chopped walnuts over each bowl.
6. Serve immediately and enjoy!

Nutritional Information: 320 calories, 12g protein, 50g carbohydrates, 8g fat, 4g fiber, 0mg cholesterol, 75mg sodium, 250mg potassium.

Note: Nutritional values are estimated based on the ingredients and serving size. Actual values may vary slightly. The final presentation of your recipe may vary slightly from the image illustration.

Greek Yogurt with Honey and Mixed Nuts

Yield: 2 servings | **Prep time:** 5 minutes | **Cook time:** 0 minutes

Ingredients:
- 2 cups Greek yogurt
- 2 tablespoons honey
- 1/4 cup mixed nuts (almonds, walnuts, pecans), chopped

Directions:
1. Divide the Greek yogurt evenly into two serving bowls.
2. Drizzle 1 tablespoon of honey over each serving of yogurt.
3. Sprinkle 2 tablespoons of mixed nuts over each bowl.
4. Serve immediately and enjoy!

Nutritional Information: 260 calories, 11g protein, 28g carbohydrates, 12g fat, 2g fiber, 0mg cholesterol, 70mg sodium, 290mg potassium.

Note: *Nutritional values are estimated based on the ingredients and serving size. Actual values may vary slightly. The final presentation of your recipe may vary slightly from the image illustration.*

Berry and Granola Parfait

Yield: 2 servings | **Prep time:** 10 minutes | **Cook time:** 0 minutes

Ingredients:
- 2 cups Greek yogurt
- 1 cup mixed berries (strawberries, blueberries, raspberries)
- 1/2 cup granola
- 2 tablespoons honey

Directions:
1. In two serving glasses or bowls, add a layer of Greek yogurt (1/2 cup each).
2. Add a layer of mixed berries (1/4 cup each) on top of the yogurt.
3. Sprinkle a layer of granola (2 tablespoons each) over the berries.
4. Repeat the layers, ending with a sprinkle of granola on top.
5. Drizzle 1 tablespoon of honey over each parfait.
6. Serve immediately and enjoy!

Nutritional Information: 350 calories, 14g protein, 50g carbohydrates, 10g fat, 5g fiber, 0mg cholesterol, 100mg sodium, 300mg potassium.

Note: *Nutritional values are estimated based on the ingredients and serving size. Actual values may vary slightly. The final presentation of your recipe may vary slightly from the image illustration.*

Shakshuka (Poached Eggs in Tomato Sauce)

Yield: 4 servings | **Prep time:** 10 minutes | **Cook time:** 20 minutes

Ingredients:

- 2 tablespoons olive oil
- 1 large onion, diced
- 1 red bell pepper, diced
- 3 cloves garlic, minced
- 1 teaspoon ground cumin
- 1 teaspoon ground paprika
- 1/4 teaspoon cayenne pepper (optional)
- 1 (28-ounce) can crushed tomatoes
- Salt and pepper to taste
- 4 large eggs
- 1/4 cup chopped fresh parsley (for garnish)

Directions:

1. Heat olive oil in a large skillet over medium heat. Add diced onion and red bell pepper, and sauté until softened, about 5-7 minutes.

2. Add minced garlic, cumin, paprika, and cayenne pepper. Cook for an additional 1-2 minutes until fragrant.

3. Pour in the crushed tomatoes and season with salt and pepper. Simmer the sauce for 10 minutes, allowing the flavors to meld and the sauce to thicken slightly.

4. Make four small wells in the tomato sauce with the back of a spoon and crack an egg into each well.

5. Cover the skillet and cook for 5-7 minutes, or until the eggs are cooked to your desired doneness.

6. Garnish with chopped fresh parsley before serving.

7. Serve immediately with crusty bread for dipping.

Nutritional Information: 180 calories, 7g protein, 12g carbohydrates, 12g fat, 4g fiber, 190mg cholesterol, 600mg sodium, 500mg potassium.

Note: *Nutritional values are estimated based on the ingredients and serving size. Actual values may vary slightly. The final presentation of your recipe may vary slightly from the image illustration.*

Spinach and Mushroom Frittata

Yield: 4 servings | **Prep time:** 10 minutes | **Cook time:** 20 minutes

Ingredients:

- 8 large eggs
- 1/4 cup milk
- 1 cup fresh spinach, chopped
- 1 cup mushrooms, sliced
- 1/2 cup shredded cheddar cheese
- 1 small onion, diced
- 1 tablespoon olive oil
- Salt and pepper to taste

Directions:

1. Preheat the oven to 350°F (175°C).

2. In a bowl, whisk together the eggs, milk, salt, and pepper until well combined.

3. Heat the olive oil in an oven-safe skillet over medium heat. Add the diced onion and sauté until softened, about 5 minutes.

4. Add the sliced mushrooms to the skillet and cook until they release their moisture and begin to brown, about 5 minutes.

5. Stir in the chopped spinach and cook until wilted, about 1-2 minutes.

6. Pour the egg mixture over the vegetables in the skillet and sprinkle the shredded cheddar cheese on top.

7. Transfer the skillet to the preheated oven and bake until the frittata is set and golden brown, about 15-20 minutes. Serve warm.

Nutritional Information: 220 calories, 14g protein, 5g carbohydrates, 16g fat, 1g fiber, 370mg cholesterol, 320mg sodium, 350mg potassium.

Note: *Nutritional values are estimated based on the ingredients and serving size. Actual values may vary slightly. The final presentation of your recipe may vary slightly from the image illustration.*

Scrambled Eggs with Smoked Salmon

Yield: 2 servings | **Prep time:** 5 minutes | **Cook time:** 5 minutes

Ingredients:
- 4 large eggs
- 1/4 cup milk
- 2 ounces smoked salmon, chopped
- 1 tablespoon butter
- Salt and pepper to taste
- Fresh chives, chopped (optional, for garnish)

Directions:
1. In a bowl, whisk together the eggs, milk, salt, and pepper until well combined.

2. Heat the butter in a non-stick skillet over medium heat.

3. Pour the egg mixture into the skillet and let it sit without stirring for about 30 seconds.

4. Gently stir the eggs with a spatula, cooking until they are softly scrambled, about 2-3 minutes.

5. Add the chopped smoked salmon to the eggs and cook for an additional 1-2 minutes until the eggs are fully cooked and the salmon is heated through.

6. Serve immediately, garnished with chopped fresh chives if desired.

Nutritional Information: 240 calories, 18g protein, 3g carbohydrates, 17g fat, 0g fiber, 410mg cholesterol, 480mg sodium, 220mg potassium.

Note: *Nutritional values are estimated based on the ingredients and serving size. Actual values may vary slightly. The final presentation of your recipe may vary slightly from the image illustration.*

Mediterranean Breakfast Wrap with Eggs and Veggies

Yield: 2 servings | **Prep time:** 10 minutes | **Cook time:** 10 minutes

Ingredients:
- 4 large eggs
- 1/4 cup milk
- 1 tablespoon olive oil
- 1/2 cup diced bell peppers (red, yellow, or green)
- 1/2 cup diced tomatoes
- 1/4 cup chopped spinach
- 1/4 cup crumbled feta cheese
- 2 large whole wheat tortillas
- Salt and pepper to taste

Directions:
1. In a bowl, whisk together the eggs, milk, salt, and pepper until well combined.

2. Heat the olive oil in a non-stick skillet over medium heat. Add the diced bell peppers and sauté until softened, about 3-4 minutes.

3. Add the diced tomatoes and chopped spinach to the skillet, cooking until the spinach is wilted, about 2 minutes.

4. Pour the egg mixture into the skillet and cook, stirring gently, until the eggs are scrambled and fully cooked, about 3-4 minutes.

5. Remove the skillet from the heat and stir in the crumbled feta cheese.

6. Divide the egg and veggie mixture between the two tortillas, placing the mixture in the center of each tortilla.

7. Roll up the tortillas tightly to form wraps. Serve immediately.

Nutritional Information: 350 calories, 20g protein, 30g carbohydrates, 15g fat, 4g fiber, 375mg cholesterol, 650mg sodium, 400mg potassium.

Note: *Nutritional values are estimated based on the ingredients and serving size. Actual values may vary slightly. The final presentation of your recipe may vary slightly from the image illustration.*

Avocado Toast with Cherry Tomatoes and Basil

Yield: 2 servings | **Prep time:** 5 minutes | **Cook time:** 0 minutes

Ingredients:

- 2 slices whole grain bread, toasted
- 1 ripe avocado
- 1/2 cup cherry tomatoes, halved
- 2 tablespoons fresh basil, chopped
- 1 tablespoon olive oil
- Salt and pepper to taste
- Lemon juice (optional, for extra flavor)

Directions:

1. Toast the slices of whole grain bread to your desired level of crispiness.
2. While the bread is toasting, cut the avocado in half, remove the pit, and scoop the flesh into a bowl. Mash the avocado with a fork until smooth.
3. Spread the mashed avocado evenly onto the toasted bread slices.
4. Top each slice with halved cherry tomatoes.
5. Sprinkle the chopped fresh basil over the tomatoes.
6. Drizzle olive oil over each slice and season with salt and pepper to taste. Add a squeeze of lemon juice if desired.
7. Serve immediately and enjoy!

Nutritional Information: 300 calories, 6g protein, 30g carbohydrates, 20g fat, 10g fiber, 0mg cholesterol, 220mg sodium, 700mg potassium.

Note: *Nutritional values are estimated based on the ingredients and serving size. Actual values may vary slightly. The final presentation of your recipe may vary slightly from the image illustration.*

Smoked Salmon and Cream Cheese Bagel

Yield: 2 servings | **Prep time:** 5 minutes | **Cook time:** 0 minutes

Ingredients:

- 2 whole grain bagels, split and toasted
- 4 ounces cream cheese, softened
- 4 ounces smoked salmon
- 1/4 cup red onion, thinly sliced
- 1/4 cup capers, drained
- Fresh dill, for garnish
- Lemon wedges, for serving (optional)

Directions:

1. Split and toast the whole grain bagels to your desired level of crispiness.
2. Spread 2 ounces of softened cream cheese on each bagel half.
3. Arrange 2 ounces of smoked salmon over the cream cheese on each bagel half.
4. Top with thinly sliced red onion and capers.
5. Garnish with fresh dill.
6. Serve with lemon wedges on the side if desired.
7. Serve immediately and enjoy!

Nutritional Information: 420 calories, 17g protein, 48g carbohydrates, 18g fat, 4g fiber, 50mg cholesterol, 780mg sodium, 350mg potassium.

Note: *Nutritional values are estimated based on the ingredients and serving size. Actual values may vary slightly. The final presentation of your recipe may vary slightly from the image illustration.*

Grilled Cheese with Spinach and Feta

Yield: 2 servings | **Prep time:** 5 minutes | **Cook time:** 10 minutes

Ingredients:

- 4 slices whole grain bread
- 1 cup fresh spinach leaves
- 1/2 cup crumbled feta cheese
- 1/2 cup shredded mozzarella cheese
- 2 tablespoons butter
- Salt and pepper to taste

Directions:

1. Heat a skillet over medium heat.
2. Spread butter on one side of each slice of bread.
3. Place two slices of bread, butter side down, in the skillet.
4. Evenly distribute the spinach leaves over the bread slices in the skillet.
5. Sprinkle the crumbled feta cheese and shredded mozzarella cheese over the spinach.
6. Season with salt and pepper to taste.
7. Top with the remaining slices of bread, butter side up.
8. Cook the sandwiches until the bread is golden brown and the cheese is melted, about 3-4 minutes per side.
9. Remove from the skillet, cut in half if desired, and serve immediately.

Nutritional Information: 450 calories, 16g protein, 40g carbohydrates, 26g fat, 4g fiber, 70mg cholesterol, 700mg sodium, 250mg potassium.

Note: *Nutritional values are estimated based on the ingredients and serving size. Actual values may vary slightly. The final presentation of your recipe may vary slightly from the image illustration.*

Tomato and Olive Tapenade Bruschetta

Yield: 4 servings | **Prep time:** 10 minutes | **Cook time:** 5 minutes

Ingredients:

- 1 baguette, sliced into 1/2-inch slices
- 1 cup cherry tomatoes, halved
- 1/2 cup black olive tapenade
- 1/4 cup fresh basil, chopped
- 2 tablespoons olive oil
- 1 garlic clove, halved
- Salt and pepper to taste

Directions:

1. Preheat the oven to 400°F (200°C).
2. Arrange the baguette slices on a baking sheet and brush with olive oil.
3. Toast the baguette slices in the oven for 5 minutes, or until golden brown.
4. Rub the toasted baguette slices with the cut side of the garlic clove.
5. Spread a thin layer of black olive tapenade on each baguette slice.
6. Top each slice with halved cherry tomatoes and sprinkle with fresh basil.
7. Season with salt and pepper to taste. Serve immediately.

Nutritional Information: 180 calories, 4g protein, 20g carbohydrates, 9g fat, 2g fiber, 0mg cholesterol, 320mg sodium, 150mg potassium.

Note: *Nutritional values are estimated based on the ingredients and serving size. Actual values may vary slightly. The final presentation of your recipe may vary slightly from the image illustration.*

Overnight Oats with Berries and Honey

Yield: 2 servings | **Prep time:** 5 minutes | **Cook time:** 0 minutes (plus overnight refrigeration)

Ingredients:
- 1 cup rolled oats
- 1 cup almond milk (or any milk of choice)
- 1/2 cup Greek yogurt
- 1/2 cup mixed berries (strawberries, blueberries, raspberries)
- 2 tablespoons honey
- 1/2 teaspoon vanilla extract
- 1/4 cup chopped nuts (optional)

Directions:
1. In a medium bowl, combine the rolled oats, almond milk, Greek yogurt, honey, and vanilla extract. Stir well to combine.
2. Divide the mixture evenly between two mason jars or bowls.
3. Top each jar with mixed berries and chopped nuts if using.
4. Cover and refrigerate overnight or for at least 6 hours.
5. In the morning, give the oats a good stir. Add additional toppings if desired.
6. Serve chilled and enjoy!

Nutritional Information: 290 calories, 10g protein, 50g carbohydrates, 6g fat, 7g fiber, 5mg cholesterol, 70mg sodium, 400mg potassium.

Note: Nutritional values are estimated based on the ingredients and serving size. Actual values may vary slightly. The final presentation of your recipe may vary slightly from the image illustration.

Quinoa Breakfast Bowl with Nuts and Fruits

Yield: 2 servings | **Prep time:** 10 minutes | **Cook time:** 15 minutes

Ingredients:
- 1 cup quinoa
- 2 cups water
- 1/2 cup almond milk (or any milk of choice)
- 1/2 teaspoon vanilla extract
- 1 tablespoon honey
- 1/2 cup mixed berries (strawberries, blueberries, raspberries)
- 1/2 cup diced apple
- 1/4 cup chopped nuts (almonds, walnuts, pecans)
- 1/4 cup dried fruits (raisins, cranberries)
- 1 tablespoon chia seeds (optional)

Directions:
1. Rinse the quinoa under cold water and drain.
2. In a medium saucepan, combine the quinoa and water. Bring to a boil, then reduce heat to low, cover, and simmer for about 15 minutes or until the quinoa is tender and water is absorbed.
3. Remove from heat and let it sit covered for 5 minutes. Fluff with a fork.
4. Divide the cooked quinoa evenly between two bowls.
5. Pour almond milk over the quinoa and stir in the vanilla extract and honey.
6. Top each bowl with mixed berries, diced apple, chopped nuts, dried fruits, and chia seeds if using.
7. Serve immediately and enjoy!

Nutritional Information: 350 calories, 10g protein, 60g carbohydrates, 12g fat, 8g fiber, 0mg cholesterol, 20mg sodium, 550mg potassium.

Note: Nutritional values are estimated based on the ingredients and serving size. Actual values may vary slightly. The final presentation of your recipe may vary slightly from the image illustration.

Warm Cinnamon Apple Oatmeal

Yield: 2 servings | **Prep time:** 5 minutes | **Cook time:** 10 minutes

Ingredients:

- 1 cup rolled oats
- 2 cups water or milk (or a combination)
- 1 apple, diced
- 1 teaspoon ground cinnamon
- 2 tablespoons honey or maple syrup
- 1/4 cup chopped walnuts or pecans
- 1/4 teaspoon salt
- 1/4 teaspoon vanilla extract (optional)

Directions:

1. In a medium saucepan, bring the water or milk to a boil.
2. Stir in the rolled oats, diced apple, ground cinnamon, and salt.
3. Reduce the heat to low and simmer, stirring occasionally, until the oats are tender and the mixture is creamy, about 10 minutes.
4. Remove from heat and stir in the honey or maple syrup and vanilla extract if using.
5. Divide the oatmeal into two bowls.
6. Top each serving with chopped walnuts or pecans.
7. Serve immediately and enjoy!

Nutritional Information: 320 calories, 7g protein, 50g carbohydrates, 10g fat, 6g fiber, 0mg cholesterol, 120mg sodium, 300mg potassium.

Note: *Nutritional values are estimated based on the ingredients and serving size. Actual values may vary slightly. The final presentation of your recipe may vary slightly from the image illustration.*

Creamy Millet Porridge with Dried Fruits

Yield: 4 servings | **Prep time:** 5 minutes | **Cook time:** 25 minutes

Ingredients:

- 1 cup millet
- 2 cups water
- 2 cups milk (or almond milk)
- 1/2 teaspoon salt
- 1/2 cup mixed dried fruits (raisins, apricots, cranberries), chopped
- 2 tablespoons honey or maple syrup
- 1 teaspoon vanilla extract
- 1/4 teaspoon ground cinnamon
- 1/4 cup chopped nuts (optional)

Directions:

1. Rinse the millet under cold water and drain.
2. In a medium saucepan, bring the water and salt to a boil. Add the millet and reduce the heat to low. Cover and simmer for 15 minutes.
3. Add the milk, dried fruits, honey or maple syrup, vanilla extract, and ground cinnamon. Stir well to combine.
4. Continue to cook over low heat, stirring occasionally, until the millet is creamy and the dried fruits are softened, about 10 minutes.
5. Remove from heat and let it sit for a few minutes to thicken.
6. Divide the porridge into four bowls.
7. Top each serving with chopped nuts if desired. Serve warm and enjoy!

Nutritional Information: 350 calories, 8g protein, 60g carbohydrates, 10g fat, 6g fiber, 0mg cholesterol, 150mg sodium, 400mg potassium.

Note: *Nutritional values are estimated based on the ingredients and serving size. Actual values may vary slightly. The final presentation of your recipe may vary slightly from the image illustration.*

Green Detox Smoothie with Spinach and Pineapple

Yield: 2 servings | **Prep time:** 5 minutes | **Cook time:** 0 minutes

Ingredients:
- 2 cups fresh spinach
- 1 cup frozen pineapple chunks
- 1 banana
- 1 cup coconut water
- 1/2 cup Greek yogurt
- 1 tablespoon chia seeds (optional)
- 1 teaspoon fresh ginger, grated (optional)
- Ice cubes (optional)

Directions:
1. In a blender, combine the fresh spinach, frozen pineapple chunks, banana, coconut water, and Greek yogurt.
2. Add the chia seeds and fresh ginger if using.
3. Blend on high speed until smooth and creamy.
4. Add ice cubes and blend again if a colder, thicker consistency is desired.
5. Divide the smoothie evenly between two glasses.
6. Serve immediately and enjoy!

Nutritional Information: 180 calories, 8g protein, 36g carbohydrates, 2g fat, 6g fiber, 5mg cholesterol, 70mg sodium, 650mg potassium.

Note: *Nutritional values are estimated based on the ingredients and serving size. Actual values may vary slightly. The final presentation of your recipe may vary slightly from the image illustration.*

Berry Banana Smoothie with Greek Yogurt

Yield: 2 servings | **Prep time:** 5 minutes | **Cook time:** 0 minutes

Ingredients:
- 1 cup mixed berries (strawberries, blueberries, raspberries)
- 1 banana
- 1 cup Greek yogurt
- 1/2 cup almond milk (or any milk of choice)
- 1 tablespoon honey
- 1/2 teaspoon vanilla extract (optional)
- Ice cubes (optional)

Directions:
1. In a blender, combine the mixed berries, banana, Greek yogurt, almond milk, and honey.
2. Add the vanilla extract if using.
3. Blend on high speed until smooth and creamy.
4. Add ice cubes and blend again if a colder, thicker consistency is desired.
5. Divide the smoothie evenly between two glasses.
6. Serve immediately and enjoy!

Nutritional Information: 220 calories, 10g protein, 40g carbohydrates, 3g fat, 5g fiber, 5mg cholesterol, 60mg sodium, 450mg potassium.

Note: *Nutritional values are estimated based on the ingredients and serving size. Actual values may vary slightly. The final presentation of your recipe may vary slightly from the image illustration.*

Mango and Turmeric Smoothie

Yield: 2 servings | **Prep time:** 5 minutes | **Cook time:** 0 minutes

Ingredients:
- 1 1/2 cups frozen mango chunks
- 1 cup coconut milk (or any milk of choice)
- 1/2 cup Greek yogurt
- 1 tablespoon honey
- 1 teaspoon ground turmeric
- 1/2 teaspoon fresh ginger, grated (optional)
- Ice cubes (optional)

Directions:
1. In a blender, combine the frozen mango chunks, coconut milk, Greek yogurt, honey, ground turmeric, and fresh ginger if using.
2. Blend on high speed until smooth and creamy.
3. Add ice cubes and blend again if a colder, thicker consistency is desired.
4. Divide the smoothie evenly between two glasses.
5. Serve immediately and enjoy!

Nutritional Information: 220 calories, 6g protein, 40g carbohydrates, 6g fat, 3g fiber, 5mg cholesterol, 50mg sodium, 400mg potassium.

Note: *Nutritional values are estimated based on the ingredients and serving size. Actual values may vary slightly. The final presentation of your recipe may vary slightly from the image illustration.*

Peach and Ginger Smoothie

Yield: 2 servings | **Prep time:** 5 minutes | **Cook time:** 0 minutes

Ingredients:
- 2 cups frozen peach slices
- 1 cup Greek yogurt
- 1/2 cup orange juice
- 1 tablespoon honey
- 1 teaspoon fresh ginger, grated
- Ice cubes (optional)

Directions:
1. In a blender, combine the frozen peach slices, Greek yogurt, orange juice, honey, and grated fresh ginger.
2. Blend on high speed until smooth and creamy.
3. Add ice cubes and blend again if a colder, thicker consistency is desired.
4. Divide the smoothie evenly between two glasses.
5. Serve immediately and enjoy!

Nutritional Information: 180 calories, 8g protein, 36g carbohydrates, 2g fat, 2g fiber, 5mg cholesterol, 45mg sodium, 450mg potassium.

Note: *Nutritional values are estimated based on the ingredients and serving size. Actual values may vary slightly. The final presentation of your recipe may vary slightly from the image illustration.*

Classic Hummus

Yield: 4 servings | **Prep time:** 10 minutes | **Cook time:** 0 minutes

Ingredients:
- 1 (15-ounce) can chickpeas, drained and rinsed
- 1/4 cup fresh lemon juice (about 1 large lemon)
- 1/4 cup well-stirred tahini
- 1 small garlic clove, minced
- 2 tablespoons extra-virgin olive oil, plus more for serving
- 1/2 teaspoon ground cumin
- Salt to taste
- 2 to 3 tablespoons water
- Dash of ground paprika, for serving

Directions:
1. In a food processor, combine the chickpeas, lemon juice, tahini, minced garlic, olive oil, ground cumin, and salt.

2. Process until smooth, about 1-2 minutes.

3. With the food processor running, add 2 to 3 tablespoons of water until the hummus reaches your desired consistency.

4. Taste and adjust seasoning as needed.

5. Transfer the hummus to a serving bowl.

6. Drizzle with additional olive oil and sprinkle with ground paprika.

7. Serve immediately with pita bread, vegetables, or as desired.

Nutritional Information: 140 calories, 4g protein, 13g carbohydrates, 8g fat, 4g fiber, 0mg cholesterol, 220mg sodium, 120mg potassium.

Note: *Nutritional values are estimated based on the ingredients and serving size. Actual values may vary slightly. The final presentation of your recipe may vary slightly from the image illustration.*

Tzatziki (Cucumber Yogurt Dip)

Yield: 4 servings | **Prep time:** 10 minutes | **Cook time:** 0 minutes

Ingredients:
- 1 cup Greek yogurt
- 1/2 large cucumber, grated and drained
- 1 tablespoon fresh lemon juice
- 1 tablespoon olive oil
- 2 cloves garlic, minced
- 1 tablespoon fresh dill, chopped
- Salt and pepper to taste

Directions:
1. Grate the cucumber and squeeze out the excess liquid using a clean kitchen towel or paper towels.

2. In a medium bowl, combine the Greek yogurt, grated cucumber, lemon juice, olive oil, minced garlic, and fresh dill.

3. Stir well to combine all the ingredients.

4. Season with salt and pepper to taste.

5. Transfer the tzatziki to a serving bowl.

6. Drizzle with a little extra olive oil if desired.

7. Serve immediately with pita bread, vegetables, or as a sauce for grilled meats.

Nutritional Information: 60 calories, 3g protein, 4g carbohydrates, 4g fat, 0g fiber, 5mg cholesterol, 60mg sodium, 150mg potassium.

Note: *Nutritional values are estimated based on the ingredients and serving size. Actual values may vary slightly. The final presentation of your recipe may vary slightly from the image illustration.*

Red Pepper and Walnut Muhammar	**Baba Ganoush (Roasted Eggplant Dip)**

Yield: 4 servings | **Prep time:** 10 minutes | **Cook time:** 0 minutes

Yield: 4 servings | **Prep time:** 10 minutes | **Cook time:** 40 minutes

Ingredients:

- 2 large red bell peppers, roasted and peeled
- 1 cup walnuts
- 2 cloves garlic, minced
- 2 tablespoons olive oil
- 1 tablespoon pomegranate molasses
- 1 teaspoon ground cumin
- 1/2 teaspoon ground paprika
- 1/4 teaspoon cayenne pepper (optional)
- Salt to taste
- Fresh parsley, chopped (for garnish)

Directions:

1. In a food processor, combine the roasted red bell peppers, walnuts, minced garlic, olive oil, pomegranate molasses, ground cumin, ground paprika, cayenne pepper (if using), and salt.

2. Process until smooth, scraping down the sides as needed.

3. Transfer the muhammar to a serving bowl.

4. Garnish with chopped fresh parsley.

5. Drizzle with a little extra olive oil if desired.

6. Serve immediately with pita bread, crackers, or fresh vegetables.

7. Enjoy your flavorful dip!

Ingredients:

- 1 large eggplant
- 1/4 cup tahini
- 2 tablespoons fresh lemon juice
- 2 tablespoons extra-virgin olive oil, plus more for serving
- 1 garlic clove, minced
- 1/2 teaspoon ground cumin
- Salt to taste
- 2 tablespoons chopped fresh parsley, for garnish
- Paprika, for garnish (optional)

Directions:

1. Preheat the oven to 400°F (200°C). Prick the eggplant a few times with a fork and place it on a baking sheet.

2. Roast the eggplant in the preheated oven for 35-40 minutes, or until it is soft and the skin is charred.

3. Remove the eggplant from the oven and let it cool slightly. Cut it open and scoop out the flesh, discarding the skin.

4. In a food processor, combine the roasted eggplant flesh, tahini, lemon juice, olive oil, minced garlic, ground cumin, and salt. Process until smooth.

5. Transfer the baba ganoush to a serving bowl.

6. Drizzle with additional olive oil and garnish with chopped fresh parsley and a sprinkle of paprika if desired.

7. Serve immediately with pita bread, vegetables, or as desired.

Nutritional Information: 180 calories, 4g protein, 9g carbohydrates, 15g fat, 4g fiber, 0mg cholesterol, 120mg sodium, 200mg potassium.

Nutritional Information: 110 calories, 2g protein, 10g carbohydrates, 7g fat, 4g fiber, 0mg cholesterol, 140mg sodium, 250mg potassium.

Note: *Nutritional values are estimated based on the ingredients and serving size. Actual values may vary slightly. The final presentation of your recipe may vary slightly from the image illustration.*

Note: *Nutritional values are estimated based on the ingredients and serving size. Actual values may vary slightly. The final presentation of your recipe may vary slightly from the image illustration.*

Date and Nut Energy Bars

Yield: 6 servings | **Prep time:** 15 minutes | **Cook time:** 0 minutes

Ingredients:
- 1 cup pitted dates
- 1/2 cup almonds
- 1/2 cup walnuts
- 1/4 cup unsweetened shredded coconut
- 2 tablespoons chia seeds
- 2 tablespoons honey
- 1/2 teaspoon vanilla extract
- 1/4 teaspoon salt

Directions:
1. In a food processor, pulse the pitted dates until they form a sticky paste.
2. Add the almonds, walnuts, shredded coconut, chia seeds, honey, vanilla extract, and salt to the food processor.
3. Pulse until the mixture is well combined and sticks together when pressed.
4. Line a baking dish with parchment paper. Press the mixture firmly into the dish to form an even layer.
5. Refrigerate for at least 1 hour to set.
6. Once set, remove from the dish and cut into bars.
7. Store in an airtight container in the refrigerator. Enjoy as a quick and healthy snack!

Nutritional Information: 210 calories, 5g protein, 26g carbohydrates, 12g fat, 4g fiber, 0mg cholesterol, 50mg sodium, 250mg potassium.

Note: *Nutritional values are estimated based on the ingredients and serving size. Actual values may vary slightly. The final presentation of your recipe may vary slightly from the image illustration.*

Oat and Honey Granola Bars

Yield: 6 servings | **Prep time:** 15 minutes | **Cook time:** 20 minutes

Ingredients:
- 2 cups rolled oats
- 1/2 cup honey
- 1/4 cup brown sugar
- 1/4 cup unsalted butter
- 1 teaspoon vanilla extract
- 1/2 teaspoon ground cinnamon
- 1/4 teaspoon salt
- 1/2 cup chopped nuts (such as almonds or walnuts)
- 1/2 cup dried fruits (such as raisins or cranberries)

Directions:
1. Preheat the oven to 350°F (175°C). Line an 8x8-inch baking dish with parchment paper.
2. In a large bowl, combine the rolled oats, chopped nuts, and dried fruits.
3. In a small saucepan over medium heat, combine the honey, brown sugar, and unsalted butter. Stir until the mixture is melted and smooth. Remove from heat and stir in the vanilla extract, ground cinnamon, and salt.
4. Pour the honey mixture over the oat mixture and stir until everything is evenly coated.
5. Press the mixture firmly into the prepared baking dish.
6. Bake in the preheated oven for 20 minutes, or until the edges are golden brown.
7. Allow the granola bars to cool completely in the dish before cutting into bars. Store in an airtight container.

Nutritional Information: 230 calories, 4g protein, 38g carbohydrates, 8g fat, 3g fiber, 10mg cholesterol, 70mg sodium, 180mg potassium.

Note: *Nutritional values are estimated based on the ingredients and serving size. Actual values may vary slightly. The final presentation of your recipe may vary slightly from the image illustration.*

Coconut and Almond Energy Balls

Yield: 6 servings | **Prep time:** 15 minutes | **Cook time:** 0 minutes

Ingredients:
- 1 cup raw almonds
- 1 cup unsweetened shredded coconut
- 1/2 cup pitted dates
- 2 tablespoons honey
- 1 tablespoon coconut oil
- 1 teaspoon vanilla extract
- 1/4 teaspoon salt

Directions:
1. In a food processor, combine the raw almonds and unsweetened shredded coconut. Pulse until finely ground.

2. Add the pitted dates, honey, coconut oil, vanilla extract, and salt to the food processor. Process until the mixture is well combined and sticks together when pressed.

3. Using your hands, roll the mixture into small balls, about 1 inch in diameter.

4. Place the energy balls on a baking sheet lined with parchment paper.

5. Refrigerate for at least 1 hour to set.

6. Store the energy balls in an airtight container in the refrigerator.

7. Enjoy as a quick and healthy snack!

Nutritional Information: 180 calories, 4g protein, 18g carbohydrates, 12g fat, 3g fiber, 0mg cholesterol, 45mg sodium, 200mg potassium.

Note: *Nutritional values are estimated based on the ingredients and serving size. Actual values may vary slightly. The final presentation of your recipe may vary slightly from the image illustration.*

Peanut Butter and Chocolate Chip Bars

Yield: 6 servings | **Prep time:** 10 minutes | **Cook time:** 20 minutes

Ingredients:
- 1 cup creamy peanut butter
- 1/2 cup honey
- 1 large egg
- 1 teaspoon vanilla extract
- 1/2 teaspoon baking soda
- 1/4 teaspoon salt
- 1 cup old-fashioned oats
- 1/2 cup mini chocolate chips

Directions:
1. Preheat the oven to 350°F (175°C). Line an 8x8-inch baking dish with parchment paper.

2. In a large bowl, combine the creamy peanut butter, honey, egg, and vanilla extract. Stir until well blended.

3. Add the baking soda and salt, and mix until combined.

4. Stir in the old-fashioned oats and mini chocolate chips until evenly distributed.

5. Press the mixture evenly into the prepared baking dish.

6. Bake in the preheated oven for 20 minutes, or until the edges are golden brown.

7. Allow to cool completely in the dish before cutting into bars. Store in an airtight container.

Nutritional Information: 250 calories, 7g protein, 30g carbohydrates, 12g fat, 3g fiber, 20mg cholesterol, 150mg sodium, 200mg potassium.

Note: *Nutritional values are estimated based on the ingredients and serving size. Actual values may vary slightly. The final presentation of your recipe may vary slightly from the image illustration.*

Grapes and Goat Cheese Platter

Yield: 4 servings | **Prep time:** 10 minutes | **Cook time:** 0 minutes

Ingredients:
- 2 cups seedless grapes (red or green), washed and dried
- 4 ounces goat cheese, sliced or crumbled
- 1/4 cup honey
- Fresh rosemary sprigs (optional, for garnish)
- Crackers or sliced baguette (optional, for serving)

Directions:
1. Arrange the grapes on a serving platter.
2. Slice or crumble the goat cheese and place it on the platter next to the grapes.
3. Drizzle honey over the goat cheese.
4. Garnish with fresh rosemary sprigs if desired.
5. Serve with crackers or sliced baguette if desired.
6. Enjoy as a snack or appetizer.

Nutritional Information: 180 calories, 5g protein, 24g carbohydrates, 7g fat, 1g fiber, 15mg cholesterol, 120mg sodium, 200mg potassium.

Note: *Nutritional values are estimated based on the ingredients and serving size. Actual values may vary slightly. The final presentation of your recipe may vary slightly from the image illustration.*

Fig and Brie Bites

Yield: 4 servings | **Prep time:** 10 minutes | **Cook time:** 0 minutes

Ingredients:
- 8 fresh figs, halved
- 4 ounces Brie cheese, cut into small pieces
- 2 tablespoons honey
- 1 tablespoon chopped fresh rosemary (optional)

Directions:
1. Arrange the fig halves on a serving platter.
2. Place a small piece of Brie cheese on top of each fig half.
3. Drizzle honey over the figs and Brie.
4. Garnish with chopped fresh rosemary if desired.
5. Serve immediately and enjoy!

Nutritional Information: 150 calories, 4g protein, 18g carbohydrates, 8g fat, 1g fiber, 20mg cholesterol, 150mg sodium, 180mg potassium.

Note: *Nutritional values are estimated based on the ingredients and serving size. Actual values may vary slightly. The final presentation of your recipe may vary slightly from the image illustration.*

Pear and Blue Cheese Salad

Yield: 4 servings | **Prep time:** 10 minutes | **Cook time:** 0 minutes

Ingredients:

- 4 cups mixed greens (such as arugula, spinach, and romaine)
- 2 ripe pears, cored and thinly sliced
- 1/2 cup crumbled blue cheese
- 1/4 cup walnuts, toasted and chopped
- 1/4 cup dried cranberries
- 3 tablespoons balsamic vinaigrette

Directions:

1. In a large salad bowl, combine the mixed greens.
2. Add the sliced pears, crumbled blue cheese, toasted walnuts, and dried cranberries.
3. Drizzle with balsamic vinaigrette.
4. Toss gently to combine.
5. Divide the salad evenly among four plates.
6. Serve immediately and enjoy!

Nutritional Information: 220 calories, 6g protein, 20g carbohydrates, 14g fat, 3g fiber, 15mg cholesterol, 200mg sodium, 280mg potassium.

Note: *Nutritional values are estimated based on the ingredients and serving size. Actual values may vary slightly. The final presentation of your recipe may vary slightly from the image illustration.*

Melon and Prosciutto Skewers

Yield: 4 servings | **Prep time:** 10 minutes | **Cook time:** 0 minutes

Ingredients:

- 1 cantaloupe, cut into 1-inch cubes
- 8 slices prosciutto, cut in half lengthwise
- 1 tablespoon balsamic glaze (optional)
- Fresh basil leaves (optional, for garnish)

Directions:

1. Cut the cantaloupe into 1-inch cubes.
2. Take each slice of prosciutto and wrap it around a cantaloupe cube.
3. Thread the prosciutto-wrapped melon onto skewers.
4. Arrange the skewers on a serving platter.
5. Drizzle with balsamic glaze if desired.
6. Garnish with fresh basil leaves if desired.
7. Serve immediately and enjoy!

Nutritional Information: 150 calories, 8g protein, 12g carbohydrates, 7g fat, 1g fiber, 25mg cholesterol, 520mg sodium, 320mg potassium.

Note: *Nutritional values are estimated based on the ingredients and serving size. Actual values may vary slightly. The final presentation of your recipe may vary slightly from the image illustration.*

Spiced Roasted Almonds

Yield: 4 servings | **Prep time:** 5 minutes | **Cook time:** 15 minutes

Ingredients:
- 2 cups raw almonds
- 1 tablespoon olive oil
- 1 teaspoon smoked paprika
- 1/2 teaspoon ground cumin
- 1/2 teaspoon garlic powder
- 1/4 teaspoon cayenne pepper (optional)
- 1/2 teaspoon salt
- 1/4 teaspoon black pepper

Directions:
1. Preheat the oven to 350°F (175°C).
2. In a medium bowl, combine the olive oil, smoked paprika, ground cumin, garlic powder, cayenne pepper (if using), salt, and black pepper.
3. Add the raw almonds to the bowl and toss to coat them evenly with the spice mixture.
4. Spread the almonds in a single layer on a baking sheet lined with parchment paper.
5. Roast in the preheated oven for 15 minutes, stirring halfway through, until the almonds are golden brown and fragrant.
6. Remove from the oven and let cool completely before serving.
7. Enjoy as a snack or appetizer.

Nutritional Information: 200 calories, 7g protein, 7g carbohydrates, 17g fat, 4g fiber, 0mg cholesterol, 150mg sodium, 240mg potassium.

Note: *Nutritional values are estimated based on the ingredients and serving size. Actual values may vary slightly. The final presentation of your recipe may vary slightly from the image illustration.*

Honey-Glazed Walnuts

Yield: 4 servings | **Prep time:** 5 minutes | **Cook time:** 10 minutes

Ingredients:
- 2 cups walnut halves
- 1/4 cup honey
- 1 tablespoon unsalted butter
- 1/2 teaspoon ground cinnamon
- 1/4 teaspoon salt

Directions:
1. Preheat the oven to 350°F (175°C). Line a baking sheet with parchment paper.
2. In a medium saucepan over medium heat, combine the honey, unsalted butter, ground cinnamon, and salt. Stir until the butter is melted and the mixture is well combined.
3. Add the walnut halves to the saucepan and stir to coat them evenly with the honey mixture.
4. Spread the coated walnuts in a single layer on the prepared baking sheet.
5. Bake in the preheated oven for 10 minutes, stirring halfway through, until the walnuts are golden brown and caramelized.
6. Remove from the oven and let cool completely before serving.
7. Serve as a snack or use as a topping for salads, oatmeal, or yogurt.

Nutritional Information: 250 calories, 4g protein, 15g carbohydrates, 20g fat, 2g fiber, 0mg cholesterol, 50mg sodium, 125mg potassium.

Note: *Nutritional values are estimated based on the ingredients and serving size. Actual values may vary slightly. The final presentation of your recipe may vary slightly from the image illustration.*

Sesame Seed Brittle

Yield: 4 servings | **Prep time:** 10 minutes | **Cook time:** 15 minutes

Ingredients:
- 1 cup sesame seeds
- 1/2 cup honey
- 1/4 cup sugar
- 1 tablespoon unsalted butter
- 1/2 teaspoon vanilla extract
- 1/4 teaspoon salt

Directions:

1. Line a baking sheet with parchment paper and set aside.

2. In a medium saucepan over medium heat, combine the honey, sugar, and unsalted butter. Stir constantly until the sugar dissolves and the mixture begins to boil.

3. Add the sesame seeds, vanilla extract, and salt to the saucepan. Stir well to combine.

4. Continue to cook, stirring frequently, until the mixture turns a deep golden brown, about 10-15 minutes.

5. Pour the hot mixture onto the prepared baking sheet and spread it out evenly using a spatula.

6. Allow the brittle to cool completely, then break it into pieces.

7. Store in an airtight container and enjoy as a sweet snack.

Nutritional Information: 210 calories, 4g protein, 24g carbohydrates, 12g fat, 3g fiber, 5mg cholesterol, 60mg sodium, 150mg potassium.

Note: *Nutritional values are estimated based on the ingredients and serving size. Actual values may vary slightly. The final presentation of your recipe may vary slightly from the image illustration.*

Rosemary Cashews

Yield: 4 servings | **Prep time:** 5 minutes | **Cook time:** 15 minutes

Ingredients:
- 2 cups raw cashews
- 2 tablespoons olive oil
- 1 tablespoon fresh rosemary, finely chopped
- 1 teaspoon salt
- 1/2 teaspoon black pepper
- 1/2 teaspoon garlic powder
- 1/4 teaspoon cayenne pepper (optional)

Directions:

1. Preheat the oven to 350°F (175°C). Line a baking sheet with parchment paper.

2. In a large bowl, combine the olive oil, chopped rosemary, salt, black pepper, garlic powder, and cayenne pepper (if using).

3. Add the raw cashews to the bowl and toss to coat them evenly with the seasoning mixture.

4. Spread the seasoned cashews in a single layer on the prepared baking sheet.

5. Roast in the preheated oven for 12-15 minutes, stirring halfway through, until the cashews are golden brown and fragrant.

6. Remove from the oven and let cool completely before serving.

7. Serve as a snack or appetizer.

Nutritional Information: 210 calories, 5g protein, 12g carbohydrates, 18g fat, 1g fiber, 0mg cholesterol, 180mg sodium, 240mg potassium.

Note: *Nutritional values are estimated based on the ingredients and serving size. Actual values may vary slightly. The final presentation of your recipe may vary slightly from the image illustration.*

Crispy Baked Zucchini Fries

Yield: 4 servings | **Prep time:** 15 minutes | **Cook time:** 20 minutes

Ingredients:

- 2 medium zucchinis, cut into fries
- 1/2 cup all-purpose flour
- 2 large eggs, beaten
- 1 cup panko breadcrumbs
- 1/2 cup grated Parmesan cheese
- 1 teaspoon garlic powder
- 1 teaspoon Italian seasoning
- Salt and pepper to taste
- Cooking spray

Directions:

1. Preheat the oven to 425°F (220°C). Line a baking sheet with parchment paper and lightly coat with cooking spray.

2. In one shallow dish, place the flour. In a second shallow dish, place the beaten eggs. In a third shallow dish, combine the panko breadcrumbs, grated Parmesan cheese, garlic powder, Italian seasoning, salt, and pepper.

3. Dredge each zucchini fry in the flour, then dip in the beaten eggs, and finally coat with the breadcrumb mixture. Place the coated zucchini fries on the prepared baking sheet.

4. Lightly spray the zucchini fries with cooking spray to help them crisp up.

5. Bake in the preheated oven for 20 minutes, flipping halfway through, until golden brown and crispy.

6. Remove from the oven and let cool slightly before serving.

7. Serve immediately with your favorite dipping sauce and enjoy!

Roasted Chickpeas with Paprika

Yield: 4 servings | **Prep time:** 5 minutes | **Cook time:** 25 minutes

Ingredients:

- 1 (15-ounce) can chickpeas, drained and rinsed
- 2 tablespoons olive oil
- 1 teaspoon smoked paprika
- 1/2 teaspoon garlic powder
- 1/2 teaspoon ground cumin
- Salt and pepper to taste

Directions:

1. Preheat the oven to 400°F (200°C).

2. Spread the drained and rinsed chickpeas on a paper towel and pat them dry.

3. In a bowl, toss the chickpeas with olive oil, smoked paprika, garlic powder, ground cumin, salt, and pepper until evenly coated.

4. Spread the seasoned chickpeas in a single layer on a baking sheet.

5. Roast in the preheated oven for 20-25 minutes, shaking the pan halfway through, until the chickpeas are golden and crispy.

6. Remove from the oven and let cool slightly before serving.

7. Serve as a snack or add to salads for extra crunch.

Nutritional Information: 180 calories, 7g protein, 22g carbohydrates, 7g fat, 2g fiber, 55mg cholesterol, 280mg sodium, 450mg potassium.

Note: *Nutritional values are estimated based on the ingredients and serving size. Actual values may vary slightly. The final presentation of your recipe may vary slightly from the image illustration.*

Nutritional Information: 150 calories, 6g protein, 18g carbohydrates, 7g fat, 6g fiber, 0mg cholesterol, 280mg sodium, 200mg potassium.

Note: *Nutritional values are estimated based on the ingredients and serving size. Actual values may vary slightly. The final presentation of your recipe may vary slightly from the image illustration.*

Carrot and Cucumber Sticks with Tahini Dip

Yield: 4 servings | **Prep time:** 15 minutes | **Cook time:** 0 minutes

Ingredients:

- 4 large carrots, peeled and cut into sticks
- 2 large cucumbers, cut into sticks
  Tahini Dip:
- 1/2 cup tahini
- 1/4 cup fresh lemon juice (about 1 large lemon)
- 2 tablespoons water
- 1 clove garlic, minced
- 1 tablespoon olive oil
- Salt and pepper to taste
- 1 tablespoon fresh parsley, chopped (optional, for garnish)

Directions:

1. Prepare the carrot and cucumber sticks and arrange them on a serving platter.

2. In a bowl, combine the tahini, fresh lemon juice, water, minced garlic, and olive oil. Stir until smooth and well combined.

3. Season the tahini dip with salt and pepper to taste.

4. Transfer the tahini dip to a serving bowl and garnish with chopped fresh parsley if desired.

5. Serve the carrot and cucumber sticks with the tahini dip.

6. Enjoy as a healthy snack or appetizer.

Marinated Artichoke Hearts

Yield: 4 servings | **Prep time:** 10 minutes | **Cook time:** 0 minutes

Ingredients:

- 1 (14-ounce) can artichoke hearts, drained and quartered
- 1/4 cup olive oil
- 2 tablespoons red wine vinegar
- 1 clove garlic, minced
- 1 teaspoon dried oregano
- 1/2 teaspoon dried basil
- 1/4 teaspoon crushed red pepper flakes (optional)
- Salt and pepper to taste
- 2 tablespoons fresh parsley, chopped (for garnish)

Directions:

1. In a medium bowl, whisk together the olive oil, red wine vinegar, minced garlic, dried oregano, dried basil, crushed red pepper flakes (if using), salt, and pepper.

2. Add the drained and quartered artichoke hearts to the bowl and toss to coat them evenly in the marinade.

3. Cover and refrigerate for at least 1 hour to allow the flavors to meld.

4. Before serving, toss the artichokes again and transfer them to a serving dish.

5. Garnish with chopped fresh parsley.

6. Serve chilled or at room temperature.

7. Enjoy as a snack, appetizer, or addition to salads.

Nutritional Information: 160 calories, 4g protein, 14g carbohydrates, 11g fat, 4g fiber, 0mg cholesterol, 90mg sodium, 350mg potassium.

Note: *Nutritional values are estimated based on the ingredients and serving size. Actual values may vary slightly. The final presentation of your recipe may vary slightly from the image illustration.*

Nutritional Information: 110 calories, 2g protein, 6g carbohydrates, 9g fat, 4g fiber, 0mg cholesterol, 290mg sodium, 240mg potassium.

Note: *Nutritional values are estimated based on the ingredients and serving size. Actual values may vary slightly. The final presentation of your recipe may vary slightly from the image illustration.*

Chickpea Salad with Cucumber and Mint

Yield: 4 servings | **Prep time:** 15 minutes | **Cook time:** 0 minutes

Ingredients:
- 2 cups cooked chickpeas (or 1 (15-ounce) can chickpeas, drained and rinsed)
- 1 cucumber, diced
- 1/4 cup red onion, finely chopped
- 1/4 cup fresh mint leaves, chopped
- 1/4 cup fresh parsley, chopped
- 1/4 cup feta cheese, crumbled
- 3 tablespoons extra-virgin olive oil
- 2 tablespoons fresh lemon juice
- 1 teaspoon ground cumin
- Salt and pepper to taste

Directions:
1. In a large salad bowl, combine the cooked chickpeas, diced cucumber, finely chopped red onion, fresh mint leaves, and fresh parsley.
2. Add the crumbled feta cheese to the bowl.
3. In a small bowl, whisk together the extra-virgin olive oil, fresh lemon juice, ground cumin, salt, and pepper.
4. Pour the dressing over the salad and toss gently to combine.
5. Adjust seasoning with additional salt and pepper if needed.
6. Serve immediately or refrigerate for later. Enjoy!

Nutritional Information: 220 calories, 7g protein, 22g carbohydrates, 12g fat, 6g fiber, 15mg cholesterol, 250mg sodium, 300mg potassium.

Note: Nutritional values are estimated based on the ingredients and serving size. Actual values may vary slightly. The final presentation of your recipe may vary slightly from the image illustration.

Lentil Salad with Feta and Herbs

Yield: 4 servings | **Prep time:** 15 minutes | **Cook time:** 20 minutes

Ingredients:
- 1 cup green or brown lentils, rinsed
- 3 cups water
- 1/2 cup red bell pepper, diced
- 1/2 cup cucumber, diced
- 1/4 cup red onion, finely chopped
- 1/4 cup fresh parsley, chopped
- 1/4 cup fresh mint, chopped
- 1/4 cup crumbled feta cheese
- 3 tablespoons extra-virgin olive oil
- 2 tablespoons fresh lemon juice
- 1 tablespoon red wine vinegar
- 1 teaspoon ground cumin
- Salt and pepper to taste

Directions:
1. In a medium saucepan, combine the lentils and water. Bring to a boil, then reduce the heat and simmer for about 20 minutes, or until the lentils are tender but not mushy. Drain and let cool to room temperature.
2. In a large salad bowl, combine the cooked lentils, red bell pepper, cucumber, red onion, fresh parsley, and fresh mint.
3. Add the crumbled feta cheese to the bowl.
4. In a small bowl, whisk together the extra-virgin olive oil, fresh lemon juice, red wine vinegar, ground cumin, salt, and pepper.
5. Pour the dressing over the salad and toss gently to combine.
6. Adjust seasoning with additional salt and pepper if needed.
7. Serve immediately or refrigerate for later. Enjoy!

Nutritional Information: 250 calories, 10g protein, 28g carbohydrates, 10g fat, 8g fiber, 15mg cholesterol, 300mg sodium, 450mg potassium.

Note: Nutritional values are estimated based on the ingredients and serving size. Actual values may vary slightly. The final presentation of your recipe may vary slightly from the image illustration.

Green Bean and Tomato Salad

Yield: 4 servings | **Prep time:** 15 minutes | **Cook time:** 5 minutes

Ingredients:

- 1 pound fresh green beans, trimmed and cut into 2-inch pieces
- 1 pint cherry tomatoes, halved
- 1/4 cup red onion, thinly sliced
- 1/4 cup fresh basil leaves, chopped
- 1/4 cup extra-virgin olive oil
- 2 tablespoons balsamic vinegar
- 1 teaspoon Dijon mustard
- Salt and pepper to taste

Directions:

1. Bring a large pot of salted water to a boil. Add the green beans and cook for about 3-5 minutes, until tender-crisp. Drain and rinse under cold water to stop the cooking process. Let cool.

2. In a large salad bowl, combine the cooked green beans, cherry tomatoes, and thinly sliced red onion.

3. Add the chopped fresh basil leaves to the bowl.

4. In a small bowl, whisk together the extra-virgin olive oil, balsamic vinegar, Dijon mustard, salt, and pepper.

5. Pour the dressing over the salad and toss gently to combine.

6. Adjust seasoning with additional salt and pepper if needed.

7. Serve immediately or refrigerate for later. Enjoy!

Nutritional Information: 150 calories, 2g protein, 12g carbohydrates, 11g fat, 4g fiber, 0mg cholesterol, 120mg sodium, 300mg potassium.

Note: *Nutritional values are estimated based on the ingredients and serving size. Actual values may vary slightly. The final presentation of your recipe may vary slightly from the image illustration.*

Red Kidney Bean Salad with Cilantro

Yield: 4 servings | **Prep time:** 15 minutes | **Cook time:** 0 minutes

Ingredients:

- 2 (15-ounce) cans red kidney beans, drained and rinsed
- 1 red bell pepper, diced
- 1/2 red onion, finely chopped
- 1/4 cup fresh cilantro, chopped
- 1/4 cup fresh lime juice
- 2 tablespoons extra-virgin olive oil
- 1 teaspoon ground cumin
- Salt and pepper to taste

Directions:

1. In a large salad bowl, combine the drained and rinsed red kidney beans, diced red bell pepper, and finely chopped red onion.

2. Add the chopped fresh cilantro to the bowl.

3. In a small bowl, whisk together the fresh lime juice, extra-virgin olive oil, ground cumin, salt, and pepper.

4. Pour the dressing over the salad and toss gently to combine.

5. Adjust seasoning with additional salt and pepper if needed.

6. Serve immediately or refrigerate for later. Enjoy!

Nutritional Information: 180 calories, 8g protein, 30g carbohydrates, 4g fat, 8g fiber, 0mg cholesterol, 240mg sodium, 350mg potassium.

Note: *Nutritional values are estimated based on the ingredients and serving size. Actual values may vary slightly. The final presentation of your recipe may vary slightly from the image illustration.*

Mediterranean Quinoa Salad

Yield: 4 servings | **Prep time:** 15 minutes | **Cook time:** 15 minutes

Ingredients:

- 1 cup quinoa, rinsed
- 2 cups water
- 1 cup cherry tomatoes, halved
- 1 cucumber, diced
- 1/2 red bell pepper, diced
- 1/4 red onion, finely chopped
- 1/2 cup Kalamata olives, pitted and halved
- 1/2 cup crumbled feta cheese
- 1/4 cup fresh parsley, chopped
- 1/4 cup extra-virgin olive oil
- 2 tablespoons fresh lemon juice
- 1 tablespoon red wine vinegar
- 1 teaspoon dried oregano
- Salt and pepper to taste

Directions:

1. In a medium saucepan, combine the rinsed quinoa and water. Bring to a boil over medium-high heat.
2. Reduce the heat to low, cover, and simmer for about 15 minutes, or until the quinoa is tender and the water is absorbed.
3. Remove the quinoa from heat and let it cool to room temperature.
4. In a large salad bowl, combine the cooled quinoa, cherry tomatoes, cucumber, red bell pepper, red onion, Kalamata olives, feta cheese, and fresh parsley.
5. In a small bowl, whisk together the extra-virgin olive oil, fresh lemon juice, red wine vinegar, dried oregano, salt, and pepper.
6. Pour the dressing over the salad and toss gently to combine.
7. Serve immediately or refrigerate for later. Enjoy!

Nutritional Information: 250 calories, 8g protein, 26g carbohydrates, 12g fat, 4g fiber, 15mg cholesterol, 300mg sodium, 400mg potassium.

Note: *Nutritional values are estimated based on the ingredients and serving size. Actual values may vary slightly. The final presentation of your recipe may vary slightly from the image illustration.*

Couscous Salad with Chickpeas and Lemon

Yield: 4 servings | **Prep time:** 10 minutes | **Cook time:** 10 minutes

Ingredients:

- 1 cup couscous
- 1 1/4 cups water
- 1 (15-ounce) can chickpeas, drained and rinsed
- 1 cup cherry tomatoes, halved
- 1 cucumber, diced
- 1/4 cup red onion, finely chopped
- 1/4 cup fresh parsley, chopped
- 1/4 cup fresh lemon juice
- 1/4 cup extra-virgin olive oil
- 1 teaspoon ground cumin
- Salt and pepper to taste

Directions:

1. In a medium saucepan, bring the water to a boil. Remove from heat, add the couscous, cover, and let it sit for 5 minutes, or until the water is absorbed. Fluff the couscous with a fork and let it cool to room temperature.
2. In a large salad bowl, combine the cooled couscous, chickpeas, cherry tomatoes, cucumber, red onion, and fresh parsley.
3. In a small bowl, whisk together the fresh lemon juice, extra-virgin olive oil, ground cumin, salt, and pepper.
4. Pour the dressing over the salad and toss gently to combine.
5. Adjust seasoning with additional salt and pepper if needed.
6. Serve immediately or refrigerate for later. Enjoy!

Nutritional Information: 220 calories, 6g protein, 30g carbohydrates, 10g fat, 5g fiber, 0mg cholesterol, 250mg sodium, 350mg potassium.

Note: *Nutritional values are estimated based on the ingredients and serving size. Actual values may vary slightly. The final presentation of your recipe may vary slightly from the image illustration.*

Brown Rice and Black Bean Salad

Yield: 4 servings | **Prep time:** 15 minutes | **Cook time:** 30 minutes

Ingredients:

- 1 cup brown rice
- 2 cups water
- 1 (15-ounce) can black beans, drained and rinsed
- 1 red bell pepper, diced
- 1 cup corn kernels (fresh or frozen)
- 1/4 cup red onion, finely chopped
- 1/4 cup fresh cilantro, chopped
- 1/4 cup fresh lime juice
- 2 tablespoons extra-virgin olive oil
- 1 teaspoon ground cumin
- Salt and pepper to taste

Directions:

1. In a medium saucepan, combine the brown rice and water. Bring to a boil, then reduce the heat to low, cover, and simmer for about 30 minutes, or until the rice is tender and the water is absorbed.

2. Fluff the rice with a fork and let it cool to room temperature.

3. In a large salad bowl, combine the cooled brown rice, black beans, diced red bell pepper, corn kernels, and red onion.

4. In a small bowl, whisk together the fresh lime juice, extra-virgin olive oil, ground cumin, salt, and pepper.

5. Pour the dressing over the salad and toss gently to combine.

6. Stir in the fresh cilantro.

7. Adjust seasoning with additional salt and pepper if needed. Serve immediately or refrigerate for later. Enjoy!

Nutritional Information: 250 calories, 7g protein, 45g carbohydrates, 7g fat, 7g fiber, 0mg cholesterol, 250mg sodium, 400mg potassium.

Note: *Nutritional values are estimated based on the ingredients and serving size. Actual values may vary slightly. The final presentation of your recipe may vary slightly from the image illustration.*

Barley Salad with Roasted Vegetables

Yield: 4 servings | **Prep time:** 15 minutes | **Cook time:** 30 minutes

Ingredients:

- 1 cup pearl barley
- 3 cups water
- 1 red bell pepper, diced
- 1 yellow bell pepper, diced
- 1 zucchini, diced
- 1 red onion, diced
- 2 tablespoons olive oil
- 1/2 teaspoon salt
- 1/4 teaspoon black pepper
- 1/4 cup feta cheese, crumbled
- 1/4 cup fresh parsley, chopped
- 2 tablespoons balsamic vinegar
- 1 tablespoon extra-virgin olive oil

Directions:

1. Preheat the oven to 400°F (200°C). Line a baking sheet with parchment paper.

2. In a medium saucepan, bring the water to a boil. Add the pearl barley, reduce heat to low, cover, and simmer for about 30 minutes, or until tender. Drain and let cool.

3. While the barley is cooking, toss the diced red bell pepper, yellow bell pepper, zucchini, and red onion with 2 tablespoons olive oil, salt, and black pepper. Spread the vegetables in a single layer on the prepared baking sheet.

4. Roast the vegetables in the preheated oven for 20-25 minutes, or until tender and slightly caramelized. Remove from the oven and let cool.

5. In a large salad bowl, combine the cooked barley and roasted vegetables.

6. Add the crumbled feta cheese and chopped fresh parsley.

7. In a small bowl, whisk together the balsamic vinegar and 1 tablespoon extra-virgin olive oil. Pour the dressing over the salad and toss gently to combine. Serve immediately or refrigerate for later. Enjoy!

Nutritional Information: 250 calories, 6g protein, 40g carbohydrates, 8g fat, 6g fiber, 10mg cholesterol, 300mg sodium, 350mg potassium.

Note: *Nutritional values are estimated based on the ingredients and serving size. Actual values may vary slightly. The final presentation of your recipe may vary slightly from the image illustration.*

Classic Greek Salad

Yield: 4 servings | **Prep time:** 15 minutes | **Cook time:** 0 minutes

Ingredients:
- 4 cups chopped romaine lettuce
- 2 cups cherry tomatoes, halved
- 1 cucumber, sliced
- 1 red onion, thinly sliced
- 1 green bell pepper, sliced
- 1/2 cup Kalamata olives, pitted
- 1/2 cup feta cheese, crumbled
- 1/4 cup extra-virgin olive oil
- 2 tablespoons red wine vinegar
- 1 teaspoon dried oregano
- Salt and pepper to taste

Directions:
1. In a large salad bowl, combine the chopped romaine lettuce, cherry tomatoes, cucumber, red onion, green bell pepper, and Kalamata olives.
2. In a small bowl, whisk together the extra-virgin olive oil, red wine vinegar, dried oregano, salt, and pepper to make the dressing.
3. Pour the dressing over the salad and toss to combine.
4. Sprinkle the crumbled feta cheese on top of the salad.
5. Toss gently to combine if desired, or leave the feta on top as a garnish.
6. Serve immediately and enjoy!

Nutritional Information: 180 calories, 5g protein, 12g carbohydrates, 14g fat, 3g fiber, 15mg cholesterol, 450mg sodium, 300mg potassium.

Note: *Nutritional values are estimated based on the ingredients and serving size. Actual values may vary slightly. The final presentation of your recipe may vary slightly from the image illustration.*

Spinach and Strawberry Salad with Balsamic Vinaigrette

Yield: 4 servings | **Prep time:** 10 minutes | **Cook time:** 0 minutes

Ingredients:
- 4 cups fresh spinach leaves
- 2 cups strawberries, hulled and sliced
- 1/4 cup red onion, thinly sliced
- 1/4 cup crumbled feta cheese
- 1/4 cup sliced almonds, toasted
  Balsamic Vinaigrette:
- 1/4 cup balsamic vinegar
- 1/4 cup extra-virgin olive oil
- 1 tablespoon honey
- 1 teaspoon Dijon mustard
- Salt and pepper to taste

Directions:
1. In a large salad bowl, combine the fresh spinach leaves, sliced strawberries, and red onion.
2. In a small bowl, whisk together the balsamic vinegar, extra-virgin olive oil, honey, Dijon mustard, salt, and pepper to make the vinaigrette.
3. Drizzle the vinaigrette over the salad and toss to combine.
4. Sprinkle the crumbled feta cheese and toasted sliced almonds on top of the salad.
5. Toss gently to combine if desired, or leave the feta and almonds on top as a garnish.
6. Serve immediately and enjoy!

Nutritional Information: 180 calories, 4g protein, 15g carbohydrates, 13g fat, 4g fiber, 10mg cholesterol, 180mg sodium, 450mg potassium.

Note: *Nutritional values are estimated based on the ingredients and serving size. Actual values may vary slightly. The final presentation of your recipe may vary slightly from the image illustration.*

Romaine Lettuce and Pomegranate Salad

Yield: 4 servings | **Prep time:** 15 minutes | **Cook time:** 0 minutes

Ingredients:

- 4 cups chopped romaine lettuce
- 1 cup pomegranate seeds
- 1/4 cup crumbled feta cheese
- 1/4 cup toasted pecans, chopped
- 1/4 cup extra-virgin olive oil
- 2 tablespoons balsamic vinegar
- 1 tablespoon honey
- Salt and pepper to taste

Directions:

1. In a large salad bowl, combine the chopped romaine lettuce, pomegranate seeds, crumbled feta cheese, and toasted pecans.
2. In a small bowl, whisk together the extra-virgin olive oil, balsamic vinegar, honey, salt, and pepper to make the dressing.
3. Drizzle the dressing over the salad.
4. Toss gently to combine, ensuring the lettuce and other ingredients are evenly coated with the dressing.
5. Adjust seasoning with additional salt and pepper if needed.
6. Serve immediately and enjoy!

Nutritional Information: 200 calories, 4g protein, 18g carbohydrates, 14g fat, 4g fiber, 10mg cholesterol, 150mg sodium, 300mg potassium.

Note: *Nutritional values are estimated based on the ingredients and serving size. Actual values may vary slightly. The final presentation of your recipe may vary slightly from the image illustration.*

Watercress Salad with Feta and Olives

Yield: 4 servings | **Prep time:** 10 minutes | **Cook time:** 0 minutes

Ingredients:

- 4 cups watercress, trimmed
- 1/2 cup crumbled feta cheese
- 1/2 cup Kalamata olives, pitted and halved
- 1/4 cup red onion, thinly sliced
- 1/4 cup extra-virgin olive oil
- 2 tablespoons fresh lemon juice
- 1 teaspoon dried oregano
- Salt and pepper to taste

Directions:

1. In a large salad bowl, combine the watercress, crumbled feta cheese, Kalamata olives, and thinly sliced red onion.
2. In a small bowl, whisk together the extra-virgin olive oil, fresh lemon juice, dried oregano, salt, and pepper to make the dressing.
3. Drizzle the dressing over the salad.
4. Toss gently to combine, ensuring the watercress and other ingredients are evenly coated with the dressing.
5. Adjust seasoning with additional salt and pepper if needed.
6. Serve immediately and enjoy!

Nutritional Information: 180 calories, 4g protein, 6g carbohydrates, 15g fat, 2g fiber, 10mg cholesterol, 280mg sodium, 250mg potassium.

Note: *Nutritional values are estimated based on the ingredients and serving size. Actual values may vary slightly. The final presentation of your recipe may vary slightly from the image illustration.*

Roasted Vegetable Salad with Balsamic Glaze

Yield: 4 servings | **Prep time:** 15 minutes | **Cook time:** 25 minutes

Ingredients:

- 2 cups cherry tomatoes, halved
- 1 red bell pepper, diced
- 1 yellow bell pepper, diced
- 1 zucchini, sliced
- 1 red onion, cut into wedges
- 3 tablespoons olive oil
- Salt and pepper to taste
- 1/4 cup balsamic vinegar
- 1 tablespoon honey
- 4 cups mixed greens (such as arugula, spinach, and romaine)

Directions:

1. Preheat the oven to 425°F (220°C). Line a baking sheet with parchment paper.

2. In a large bowl, toss the cherry tomatoes, red bell pepper, yellow bell pepper, zucchini, and red onion with olive oil, salt, and pepper.

3. Spread the vegetables in a single layer on the prepared baking sheet.

4. Roast in the preheated oven for 20-25 minutes, or until the vegetables are tender and slightly caramelized. Remove from the oven and let cool slightly.

5. While the vegetables are roasting, combine the balsamic vinegar and honey in a small saucepan over medium heat. Bring to a simmer and cook until the mixture is reduced by half and thickened into a glaze, about 5-7 minutes.

6. In a large salad bowl, combine the mixed greens with the roasted vegetables.

7. Drizzle the balsamic glaze over the salad and toss gently to combine. Adjust seasoning with additional salt and pepper if needed. Serve immediately and enjoy!

Nutritional Information: 200 calories, 4g protein, 22g carbohydrates, 12g fat, 5g fiber, 0mg cholesterol, 150mg sodium, 600mg potassium.

Note: *Nutritional values are estimated based on the ingredients and serving size. Actual values may vary slightly. The final presentation of your recipe may vary slightly from the image illustration.*

Grilled Zucchini and Bell Pepper Salad

Yield: 4 servings | **Prep time:** 15 minutes | **Cook time:** 10 minutes

Ingredients:

- 2 medium zucchinis, sliced lengthwise
- 1 red bell pepper, quartered and seeded
- 1 yellow bell pepper, quartered and seeded
- 1/4 cup extra-virgin olive oil, divided
- Salt and pepper to taste
- 2 tablespoons balsamic vinegar
- 1 clove garlic, minced
- 1/4 cup fresh basil leaves, chopped
- 4 cups mixed greens (such as arugula, spinach, and romaine)

Directions:

1. Preheat a grill to medium-high heat.

2. Brush the zucchini slices and bell pepper quarters with 2 tablespoons of olive oil and season with salt and pepper.

3. Grill the zucchini and bell peppers for 3-4 minutes on each side, until tender and slightly charred. Remove from the grill and let cool slightly.

4. Cut the grilled zucchini slices and bell pepper quarters into bite-sized pieces.

5. In a small bowl, whisk together the remaining 2 tablespoons of olive oil, balsamic vinegar, minced garlic, salt, and pepper.

6. In a large salad bowl, combine the mixed greens, grilled zucchini, and grilled bell peppers.

7. Drizzle the dressing over the salad and toss gently to combine. Sprinkle with fresh basil leaves. Serve immediately and enjoy!

Nutritional Information: 180 calories, 3g protein, 12g carbohydrates, 14g fat, 4g fiber, 0mg cholesterol, 150mg sodium, 550mg potassium.

Note: *Nutritional values are estimated based on the ingredients and serving size. Actual values may vary slightly. The final presentation of your recipe may vary slightly from the image illustration.*

Mediterranean Veggie Salad with Olives

Yield: 4 servings | **Prep time:** 15 minutes | **Cook time:** 0 minutes

Ingredients:
- 1 cup cherry tomatoes, halved
- 1 large cucumber, diced
- 1 red bell pepper, diced
- 1 yellow bell pepper, diced
- 1/2 red onion, thinly sliced
- 1/2 cup Kalamata olives, pitted and halved
- 1/4 cup fresh parsley, chopped
- 1/4 cup extra-virgin olive oil
- 2 tablespoons red wine vinegar
- 1 teaspoon dried oregano
- Salt and pepper to taste

Directions:
1. In a large salad bowl, combine the cherry tomatoes, diced cucumber, red bell pepper, yellow bell pepper, and thinly sliced red onion.
2. Add the halved Kalamata olives and chopped fresh parsley to the bowl.
3. In a small bowl, whisk together the extra-virgin olive oil, red wine vinegar, dried oregano, salt, and pepper.
4. Pour the dressing over the salad and toss gently to combine.
5. Adjust seasoning with additional salt and pepper if needed.
6. Serve immediately and enjoy!

Nutritional Information: 150 calories, 2g protein, 12g carbohydrates, 11g fat, 3g fiber, 0mg cholesterol, 300mg sodium, 350mg potassium.

Note: *Nutritional values are estimated based on the ingredients and serving size. Actual values may vary slightly. The final presentation of your recipe may vary slightly from the image illustration.*

Roasted Beet and Goat Cheese Salad

Yield: 4 servings | **Prep time:** 15 minutes | **Cook time:** 40 minutes

Ingredients:
- 4 medium beets, peeled and diced
- 2 tablespoons olive oil
- Salt and pepper to taste
- 4 cups mixed greens (such as arugula, spinach, and romaine)
- 1/4 cup walnuts, toasted and chopped
- 1/4 cup crumbled goat cheese
- 2 tablespoons balsamic vinegar
- 2 tablespoons extra-virgin olive oil
- 1 teaspoon honey
- Salt and pepper to taste

Directions:
1. Preheat the oven to 400°F (200°C). Line a baking sheet with parchment paper.
2. Toss the diced beets with 2 tablespoons of olive oil, salt, and pepper. Spread evenly on the prepared baking sheet.
3. Roast the beets in the preheated oven for 35-40 minutes, or until tender and slightly caramelized. Remove from the oven and let cool slightly.
4. In a large salad bowl, combine the mixed greens, roasted beets, toasted walnuts, and crumbled goat cheese.
5. In a small bowl, whisk together the balsamic vinegar, extra-virgin olive oil, honey, salt, and pepper.
6. Pour the dressing over the salad and toss gently to combine.
7. Adjust seasoning with additional salt and pepper if needed. Serve immediately and enjoy!

Nutritional Information: 250 calories, 5g protein, 20g carbohydrates, 18g fat, 5g fiber, 10mg cholesterol, 300mg sodium, 400mg potassium.

Note: *Nutritional values are estimated based on the ingredients and serving size. Actual values may vary slightly. The final presentation of your recipe may vary slightly from the image illustration.*

Carrot and Raisin Salad with Orange Dressing

Yield: 4 servings | **Prep time:** 15 minutes | **Cook time:** 0 minutes

Ingredients:

- 4 large carrots, peeled and grated
- 1/2 cup raisins
- 1/4 cup chopped walnuts
- 1/4 cup fresh parsley, chopped
- 1/4 cup fresh orange juice
- 2 tablespoons extra-virgin olive oil
- 1 tablespoon honey
- 1 teaspoon orange zest
- Salt and pepper to taste

Directions:

1. In a large salad bowl, combine the grated carrots, raisins, chopped walnuts, and chopped fresh parsley.
2. In a small bowl, whisk together the fresh orange juice, extra-virgin olive oil, honey, orange zest, salt, and pepper.
3. Pour the dressing over the salad and toss gently to combine.
4. Adjust seasoning with additional salt and pepper if needed.
5. Serve immediately or refrigerate for later. Enjoy!

Nutritional Information: 180 calories, 2g protein, 22g carbohydrates, 10g fat, 3g fiber, 0mg cholesterol, 50mg sodium, 300mg potassium.

Note: Nutritional values are estimated based on the ingredients and serving size. Actual values may vary slightly. The final presentation of your recipe may vary slightly from the image illustration.

Eggplant and Tomato Salad with Garlic Yogurt

Yield: 4 servings | **Prep time:** 20 minutes | **Cook time:** 20 minutes

Ingredients:

- 2 medium eggplants, diced
- 1/4 cup olive oil, divided
- Salt and pepper to taste
- 2 large tomatoes, diced
- 1/4 cup red onion, thinly sliced
- 1/4 cup fresh parsley, chopped
- 1 cup plain Greek yogurt
- 2 cloves garlic, minced
- 1 tablespoon lemon juice

Directions:

1. Preheat the oven to 400°F (200°C). Line a baking sheet with parchment paper.
2. Toss the diced eggplants with 2 tablespoons of olive oil, salt, and pepper. Spread evenly on the prepared baking sheet.
3. Roast the eggplants in the preheated oven for 20 minutes, or until tender and slightly caramelized. Remove from the oven and let cool slightly.
4. In a large salad bowl, combine the roasted eggplant, diced tomatoes, thinly sliced red onion, and chopped fresh parsley.
5. In a small bowl, mix the plain Greek yogurt, minced garlic, lemon juice, remaining 2 tablespoons of olive oil, salt, and pepper.
6. Pour the garlic yogurt dressing over the salad and toss gently to combine.
7. Adjust seasoning with additional salt and pepper if needed. Serve immediately and enjoy!

Nutritional Information: 220 calories, 6g protein, 18g carbohydrates, 14g fat, 6g fiber, 5mg cholesterol, 150mg sodium, 500mg potassium.

Note: Nutritional values are estimated based on the ingredients and serving size. Actual values may vary slightly. The final presentation of your recipe may vary slightly from the image illustration.

Shrimp and Avocado Salad

Yield: 4 servings | **Prep time:** 15 minutes | **Cook time:** 10 minutes

Ingredients:

- 1 pound large shrimp, peeled and deveined
- 1 tablespoon olive oil
- Salt and pepper to taste
- 2 ripe avocados, diced
- 1 cup cherry tomatoes, halved
- 1/2 cucumber, diced
- 1/4 red onion, thinly sliced
- 1/4 cup fresh cilantro, chopped
- 1/4 cup fresh lime juice
- 2 tablespoons extra-virgin olive oil
- 1 teaspoon ground cumin
- Salt and pepper to taste

Directions:

1. Heat 1 tablespoon of olive oil in a large skillet over medium heat. Season the shrimp with salt and pepper, then add them to the skillet.

2. Cook the shrimp for 2-3 minutes on each side, until they are pink and opaque. Remove from heat and let cool slightly.

3. In a large salad bowl, combine the diced avocados, cherry tomatoes, cucumber, thinly sliced red onion, and fresh cilantro.

4. Add the cooked shrimp to the bowl.

5. In a small bowl, whisk together the fresh lime juice, extra-virgin olive oil, ground cumin, salt, and pepper.

6. Pour the dressing over the salad and toss gently to combine.

7. Adjust seasoning with additional salt and pepper if needed. Serve immediately and enjoy!

Nutritional Information: 350 calories, 25g protein, 14g carbohydrates, 24g fat, 7g fiber, 220mg cholesterol, 450mg sodium, 500mg potassium.

Note: *Nutritional values are estimated based on the ingredients and serving size. Actual values may vary slightly. The final presentation of your recipe may vary slightly from the image illustration.*

Grilled Octopus Salad with Potatoes

Yield: 4 servings | **Prep time:** 20 minutes | **Cook time:** 40 minutes

Ingredients:

- 2 pounds octopus, cleaned
- 4 large potatoes, peeled and diced
- 1/4 cup extra-virgin olive oil, divided
- 2 tablespoons fresh lemon juice
- 2 cloves garlic, minced
- 1/4 cup fresh parsley, chopped
- 1/2 cup cherry tomatoes, halved
- 1/4 cup red onion, thinly sliced
- Salt and pepper to taste

Directions:

1. Bring a large pot of water to a boil. Add the octopus and cook for about 30-40 minutes, or until tender. Remove from water and let cool slightly.

2. While the octopus is cooking, bring another pot of salted water to a boil. Add the diced potatoes and cook until tender, about 10-15 minutes. Drain and let cool.

3. Preheat a grill to medium-high heat. Brush the octopus with 2 tablespoons of olive oil and season with salt and pepper. Grill the octopus for about 2-3 minutes on each side, until slightly charred. Remove from grill and cut into bite-sized pieces.

4. In a large salad bowl, combine the cooked potatoes, grilled octopus, cherry tomatoes, and thinly sliced red onion.

5. In a small bowl, whisk together the remaining 2 tablespoons of olive oil, fresh lemon juice, minced garlic, salt, and pepper.

6. Pour the dressing over the salad and toss gently to combine.

7. Sprinkle with fresh parsley and adjust seasoning with additional salt and pepper if needed. Serve immediately and enjoy!

Nutritional Information: 350 calories, 20g protein, 35g carbohydrates, 14g fat, 4g fiber, 100mg cholesterol, 400mg sodium, 750mg potassium.

Note: *Nutritional values are estimated based on the ingredients and serving size. Actual values may vary slightly. The final presentation of your recipe may vary slightly from the image illustration.*

Smoked Salmon and Dill Salad

Yield: 4 servings | **Prep time:** 15 minutes | **Cook time:** 0 minutes

Ingredients:
- 8 ounces smoked salmon, sliced
- 4 cups mixed greens (such as arugula, spinach, and romaine)
- 1 cup cherry tomatoes, halved
- 1/2 cucumber, thinly sliced
- 1/4 red onion, thinly sliced
- 1/4 cup fresh dill, chopped
- 1/4 cup extra-virgin olive oil
- 2 tablespoons fresh lemon juice
- 1 teaspoon Dijon mustard
- Salt and pepper to taste

Directions:
1. In a large salad bowl, arrange the mixed greens, cherry tomatoes, thinly sliced cucumber, and thinly sliced red onion.
2. Add the sliced smoked salmon to the bowl.
3. In a small bowl, whisk together the extra-virgin olive oil, fresh lemon juice, Dijon mustard, salt, and pepper.
4. Pour the dressing over the salad and toss gently to combine.
5. Sprinkle the chopped fresh dill over the top of the salad.
6. Adjust seasoning with additional salt and pepper if needed.
7. Serve immediately and enjoy!

Nutritional Information: 250 calories, 15g protein, 10g carbohydrates, 18g fat, 2g fiber, 30mg cholesterol, 450mg sodium, 350mg potassium.

Note: *Nutritional values are estimated based on the ingredients and serving size. Actual values may vary slightly. The final presentation of your recipe may vary slightly from the image illustration.*

Calamari Salad with Olives and Capers

Yield: 4 servings | **Prep time:** 15 minutes | **Cook time:** 10 minutes

Ingredients:
- 1 pound calamari, cleaned and cut into rings
- 1/4 cup extra-virgin olive oil, divided
- 2 cloves garlic, minced
- 1/2 cup black olives, pitted and halved
- 2 tablespoons capers, rinsed
- 1/2 cup cherry tomatoes, halved
- 1/4 cup red onion, thinly sliced
- 1/4 cup fresh parsley, chopped
- 2 tablespoons fresh lemon juice
- Salt and pepper to taste

Directions:
1. Heat 2 tablespoons of olive oil in a large skillet over medium-high heat. Add the minced garlic and sauté for 1 minute.
2. Add the calamari rings to the skillet and cook for 3-4 minutes, until they are opaque and tender. Remove from heat and let cool slightly.
3. In a large salad bowl, combine the cooked calamari, black olives, capers, cherry tomatoes, and thinly sliced red onion.
4. Add the chopped fresh parsley to the bowl.
5. In a small bowl, whisk together the remaining 2 tablespoons of olive oil, fresh lemon juice, salt, and pepper.
6. Pour the dressing over the salad and toss gently to combine.
7. Adjust seasoning with additional salt and pepper if needed. Serve immediately and enjoy!

Nutritional Information: 220 calories, 18g protein, 6g carbohydrates, 14g fat, 2g fiber, 180mg cholesterol, 500mg sodium, 400mg potassium.

Note: *Nutritional values are estimated based on the ingredients and serving size. Actual values may vary slightly. The final presentation of your recipe may vary slightly from the image illustration.*

Crab and Mango Salad

Yield: 4 servings | **Prep time:** 20 minutes | **Cook time:** 0 minutes

Ingredients:

- 1 pound fresh crab meat, picked over for shells
- 2 ripe mangoes, peeled and diced
- 1/2 red bell pepper, diced
- 1/2 avocado, diced
- 1/4 cup red onion, finely chopped
- 1/4 cup fresh cilantro, chopped
- 1/4 cup fresh lime juice
- 2 tablespoons extra-virgin olive oil
- 1 teaspoon honey
- Salt and pepper to taste

Directions:

1. In a large salad bowl, combine the fresh crab meat, diced mangoes, diced red bell pepper, diced avocado, and finely chopped red onion.
2. Add the chopped fresh cilantro to the bowl.
3. In a small bowl, whisk together the fresh lime juice, extra-virgin olive oil, honey, salt, and pepper.
4. Pour the dressing over the salad and toss gently to combine.
5. Adjust seasoning with additional salt and pepper if needed.
6. Serve immediately and enjoy!

Nutritional Information: 220 calories, 20g protein, 20g carbohydrates, 8g fat, 4g fiber, 80mg cholesterol, 300mg sodium, 400mg potassium.

Note: *Nutritional values are estimated based on the ingredients and serving size. Actual values may vary slightly. The final presentation of your recipe may vary slightly from the image illustration.*

Scallop and Mango Salad

Yield: 4 servings | **Prep time:** 15 minutes | **Cook time:** 10 minutes

Ingredients:

- 1 pound large sea scallops
- 2 tablespoons olive oil
- Salt and pepper to taste
- 2 mangoes, diced
- 1 avocado, diced
- 1/2 red onion, thinly sliced
- 1/4 cup fresh mint leaves, chopped
- 1/4 cup fresh lime juice
- 2 tablespoons extra-virgin olive oil
- 1 teaspoon honey
- Salt and pepper to taste

Directions:

1. Pat the scallops dry with paper towels. Season with salt and pepper.
2. Heat 2 tablespoons of olive oil in a large skillet over medium-high heat. Add the scallops and cook for 2-3 minutes on each side, until golden brown and opaque. Remove from heat and let cool slightly.
3. In a large salad bowl, combine the diced mangoes, diced avocado, thinly sliced red onion, and chopped fresh mint leaves.
4. Add the cooked scallops to the bowl.
5. In a small bowl, whisk together the fresh lime juice, extra-virgin olive oil, honey, salt, and pepper.
6. Pour the dressing over the salad and toss gently to combine.
7. Adjust seasoning with additional salt and pepper if needed. Serve immediately and enjoy!

Nutritional Information: 280 calories, 18g protein, 20g carbohydrates, 16g fat, 6g fiber, 40mg cholesterol, 400mg sodium, 600mg potassium.

Note: *Nutritional values are estimated based on the ingredients and serving size. Actual values may vary slightly. The final presentation of your recipe may vary slightly from the image illustration.*

Quinoa Bowl with Roasted Vegetables and Feta

Yield: 4 servings | **Prep time:** 15 minutes | **Cook time:** 30 minutes

Ingredients:

- 1 cup quinoa, rinsed
- 2 cups water
- 1 red bell pepper, chopped
- 1 zucchini, chopped
- 1 yellow squash, chopped
- 1 red onion, chopped
- 2 tablespoons olive oil
- 1 teaspoon dried oregano
- Salt and pepper to taste
- 1 cup cherry tomatoes, halved
- 1/2 cup crumbled feta cheese
- 2 tablespoons fresh parsley, chopped
- 1 lemon, juiced

Directions:

1. Preheat the oven to 425°F (220°C).

2. In a medium pot, bring the quinoa and water to a boil. Reduce the heat to low, cover, and simmer for 15 minutes or until the quinoa is cooked and the water is absorbed. Fluff with a fork and set aside.

3. While the quinoa is cooking, place the chopped red bell pepper, zucchini, yellow squash, and red onion on a baking sheet. Drizzle with olive oil, sprinkle with dried oregano, and season with salt and pepper. Toss to coat.

4. Roast the vegetables in the preheated oven for 20-25 minutes, or until tender and slightly caramelized.

5. In a large bowl, combine the cooked quinoa, roasted vegetables, cherry tomatoes, crumbled feta cheese, and fresh parsley. Drizzle with lemon juice and toss to combine.

6. Season with additional salt and pepper to taste, if needed.

7. Serve warm or at room temperature.

Nutritional Information: 290 calories, 10g protein, 36g carbohydrates, 12g fat, 6g fiber, 20mg cholesterol, 350mg sodium, 450mg potassium.

Note: *Nutritional values are estimated based on the ingredients and serving size. Actual values may vary slightly. The final presentation of your recipe may vary slightly from the image illustration.*

Brown Rice Bowl with Grilled Chicken and Avocado

Yield: 4 servings | **Prep time:** 15 minutes | **Cook time:** 30 minutes

Ingredients:

- 1 cup brown rice
- 2 cups water or chicken broth
- 1 pound boneless, skinless chicken breasts
- 2 tablespoons olive oil, divided
- 1 teaspoon garlic powder
- 1 teaspoon paprika
- Salt and pepper to taste
- 2 avocados, sliced
- 1 cup cherry tomatoes, halved
- 1/4 cup red onion, finely chopped
- 2 tablespoons fresh lime juice
- 1/4 cup fresh cilantro, chopped

Directions:

1. In a medium pot, bring the brown rice and water or chicken broth to a boil. Reduce the heat to low, cover, and simmer for 30 minutes or until the rice is tender and the liquid is absorbed. Fluff with a fork and set aside.

2. While the rice is cooking, preheat the grill to medium-high heat. Rub the chicken breasts with 1 tablespoon of olive oil, garlic powder, paprika, salt, and pepper.

3. Grill the chicken for 6-8 minutes per side, or until fully cooked and the internal temperature reaches 165°F (74°C). Remove from the grill and let rest for 5 minutes before slicing.

4. In a large bowl, combine the cooked brown rice, sliced grilled chicken, avocado slices, cherry tomatoes, and red onion.

5. Drizzle with the remaining 1 tablespoon of olive oil and fresh lime juice. Toss to combine.

6. Garnish with fresh cilantro and season with additional salt and pepper to taste, if needed.

7. Serve warm or at room temperature.

Nutritional Information: 450 calories, 30g protein, 40g carbohydrates, 20g fat, 8g fiber, 70mg cholesterol, 400mg sodium, 700mg potassium.

Note: *Nutritional values are estimated based on the ingredients and serving size. Actual values may vary slightly. The final presentation of your recipe may vary slightly from the image illustration.*

Barley Bowl with Mushrooms and Spinach

Yield: 4 servings | **Prep time:** 10 minutes | **Cook time:** 35 minutes

Ingredients:

- 1 cup pearl barley
- 3 cups water or vegetable broth
- 2 tablespoons olive oil
- 1 large onion, chopped
- 3 cloves garlic, minced
- 8 ounces mushrooms, sliced
- 4 cups fresh spinach
- 1 teaspoon dried thyme
- Salt and pepper to taste
- 1/4 cup grated Parmesan cheese (optional)

Directions:

1. In a medium pot, bring the barley and water or vegetable broth to a boil. Reduce the heat to low, cover, and simmer for 25-30 minutes or until the barley is tender and the liquid is absorbed. Drain any excess liquid and set aside.

2. In a large skillet, heat the olive oil over medium heat. Add the chopped onion and cook until softened, about 5 minutes.

3. Stir in the minced garlic and cook for another 1-2 minutes until fragrant.

4. Add the sliced mushrooms and cook until they release their moisture and become tender, about 5-7 minutes.

5. Stir in the fresh spinach and cook until wilted, about 2-3 minutes.

6. Add the cooked barley to the skillet and stir to combine. Season with dried thyme, salt, and pepper to taste.

7. If desired, sprinkle with grated Parmesan cheese before serving.

Nutritional Information: 320 calories, 10g protein, 52g carbohydrates, 9g fat, 9g fiber, 5mg cholesterol, 250mg sodium, 600mg potassium.

Note: *Nutritional values are estimated based on the ingredients and serving size. Actual values may vary slightly. The final presentation of your recipe may vary slightly from the image illustration.*

Couscous Bowl with Chickpeas and Mint

Yield: 4 servings | **Prep time:** 10 minutes | **Cook time:** 10 minutes

Ingredients:

- 1 cup couscous
- 1 cup boiling water or vegetable broth
- 1 can (15 ounces) chickpeas, drained and rinsed
- 1/4 cup red onion, finely chopped
- 1/2 cup cherry tomatoes, halved
- 1/4 cup fresh mint leaves, chopped
- 1/4 cup fresh parsley, chopped
- 2 tablespoons olive oil
- 2 tablespoons fresh lemon juice
- Salt and pepper to taste

Directions:

1. In a large bowl, combine the couscous and boiling water or vegetable broth. Cover and let sit for 5 minutes, or until the liquid is absorbed. Fluff with a fork.

2. Add the chickpeas, red onion, cherry tomatoes, mint, and parsley to the couscous.

3. In a small bowl, whisk together the olive oil and lemon juice. Pour over the couscous mixture and toss to combine.

4. Season with salt and pepper to taste.

5. Serve warm or at room temperature.

Nutritional Information: 280 calories, 8g protein, 44g carbohydrates, 8g fat, 8g fiber, 0mg cholesterol, 320mg sodium, 400mg potassium.

Note: *Nutritional values are estimated based on the ingredients and serving size. Actual values may vary slightly. The final presentation of your recipe may vary slightly from the image illustration.*

Wild Rice Bowl with Salmon and Asparagus

Yield: 4 servings | **Prep time:** 15 minutes | **Cook time:** 30 minutes

Ingredients:
- 1 cup wild rice
- 3 cups water or vegetable broth
- 1 pound salmon fillets
- 1 bunch asparagus, trimmed and cut into 2-inch pieces
- 2 tablespoons olive oil, divided
- 1 lemon, sliced
- 1 teaspoon garlic powder
- Salt and pepper to taste
- 1/4 cup fresh dill, chopped

Directions:

1. In a medium pot, bring the wild rice and water or vegetable broth to a boil. Reduce the heat to low, cover, and simmer for 30-35 minutes or until the rice is tender and the liquid is absorbed. Drain any excess liquid and set aside.

2. Preheat the oven to 400°F (200°C). Line a baking sheet with parchment paper.

3. Place the salmon fillets on one side of the baking sheet and the asparagus on the other. Drizzle both with 1 tablespoon of olive oil, and season with garlic powder, salt, and pepper. Arrange lemon slices over the salmon.

4. Roast in the preheated oven for 15-20 minutes, or until the salmon is cooked through and flakes easily with a fork, and the asparagus is tender.

5. In a large bowl, combine the cooked wild rice, roasted asparagus, and flaked salmon (remove lemon slices). Drizzle with the remaining 1 tablespoon of olive oil and sprinkle with fresh dill.

6. Toss gently to combine all ingredients.

7. Serve warm or at room temperature.

Nutritional Information: 450 calories, 28g protein, 38g carbohydrates, 18g fat, 6g fiber, 70mg cholesterol, 320mg sodium, 700mg potassium.

Note: Nutritional values are estimated based on the ingredients and serving size. Actual values may vary slightly. The final presentation of your recipe may vary slightly from the image illustration.

Bulgur Bowl with Tomatoes and Cucumbers

Yield: 4 servings | **Prep time:** 10 minutes | **Cook time:** 15 minutes

Ingredients:
- 1 cup bulgur wheat
- 2 cups water or vegetable broth
- 1 cup cherry tomatoes, halved
- 1 large cucumber, diced
- 1/4 cup red onion, finely chopped
- 1/4 cup fresh parsley, chopped
- 1/4 cup fresh mint, chopped
- 3 tablespoons olive oil
- 2 tablespoons fresh lemon juice
- Salt and pepper to taste

Directions:

1. In a medium pot, bring the water or vegetable broth to a boil. Stir in the bulgur wheat, cover, and remove from heat. Let sit for 10-15 minutes, or until the liquid is absorbed and the bulgur is tender. Fluff with a fork and set aside to cool slightly.

2. In a large bowl, combine the cooked bulgur, cherry tomatoes, cucumber, red onion, parsley, and mint.

3. In a small bowl, whisk together the olive oil and lemon juice. Pour over the bulgur mixture and toss to combine.

4. Season with salt and pepper to taste.

5. Serve the bulgur bowl at room temperature or chilled.

Nutritional Information: 250 calories, 6g protein, 35g carbohydrates, 10g fat, 6g fiber, 0mg cholesterol, 220mg sodium, 450mg potassium.

Note: Nutritional values are estimated based on the ingredients and serving size. Actual values may vary slightly. The final presentation of your recipe may vary slightly from the image illustration.

Baked Salmon with Dill and Lemon

Yield: 4 servings | **Prep time:** 10 minutes | **Cook time:** 20 minutes

Ingredients:

- 4 salmon fillets (6 oz each)
- 2 tablespoons olive oil
- 2 tablespoons fresh lemon juice
- 1 tablespoon lemon zest
- 2 cloves garlic, minced
- 2 tablespoons fresh dill, chopped
- Salt and pepper to taste
- Lemon slices for garnish

Directions:

1. Preheat the oven to 375°F.

2. In a small bowl, mix together the olive oil, lemon juice, lemon zest, minced garlic, and chopped dill.

3. Place the salmon fillets on a baking sheet lined with parchment paper. Season with salt and pepper.

4. Brush the dill and lemon mixture over the salmon fillets, making sure they are well coated.

5. Arrange lemon slices on top of each fillet.

6. Bake in the preheated oven for 20 minutes, or until the salmon flakes easily with a fork.

7. Serve warm, garnished with additional dill if desired.

Chicken Souvlaki with Tzatziki

Yield: 4 servings | **Prep time:** 20 minutes | **Cook time:** 15 minutes

Ingredients:

- 1.5 lbs chicken breast, cut into 1-inch cubes
- 1/4 cup olive oil
- 3 tablespoons fresh lemon juice
- 3 cloves garlic, minced
- 2 tablespoons dried oregano
- Salt and pepper to taste
- 1 cup plain Greek yogurt
- 1/2 cucumber, grated
- 1 tablespoon fresh dill, chopped
- 1 tablespoon fresh lemon juice
- 2 cloves garlic, minced
- Salt to taste

Directions:

1. In a bowl, combine olive oil, lemon juice, garlic, oregano, salt, and pepper. Add chicken cubes and marinate for at least 15 minutes.

2. Preheat grill to medium-high heat.

3. Thread chicken onto skewers and grill for 10-15 minutes, turning occasionally, until fully cooked.

4. For the tzatziki, mix Greek yogurt, grated cucumber, dill, lemon juice, garlic, and salt in a bowl.

5. Serve grilled chicken skewers with a side of tzatziki sauce.

6. Optionally, garnish with additional fresh dill or lemon wedges.

7. Serve warm with pita bread and fresh vegetables.

Nutritional Information: 350 calories, 35g protein, 2g carbohydrates, 22g fat, 0g fiber, 95mg cholesterol, 240mg sodium, 420mg potassium.

Note: *Nutritional values are estimated based on the ingredients and serving size. Actual values may vary slightly. The final presentation of your recipe may vary slightly from the image illustration.*

Nutritional Information: 380 calories, 34g protein, 10g carbohydrates, 22g fat, 1g fiber, 90mg cholesterol, 360mg sodium, 450mg potassium.

Note: *Nutritional values are estimated based on the ingredients and serving size. Actual values may vary slightly. The final presentation of your recipe may vary slightly from the image illustration.*

Fish Tacos with Lime and Cilantro

Yield: 4 servings | **Prep time:** 15 minutes | **Cook time:** 10 minutes

Ingredients:
- 1 lb white fish fillets (such as cod or tilapia)
- 2 tablespoons olive oil
- 2 tablespoons lime juice
- 1 teaspoon chili powder
- 1/2 teaspoon ground cumin
- Salt and pepper to taste
- 8 small corn tortillas
- 1 cup shredded cabbage
- 1/2 cup chopped cilantro
- 1/4 cup thinly sliced red onion
- Lime wedges for serving

Directions:
1. Preheat grill or skillet over medium-high heat.
2. In a bowl, mix olive oil, lime juice, chili powder, cumin, salt, and pepper. Brush mixture over fish fillets.
3. Cook fish for 3-4 minutes per side until opaque and flakes easily with a fork.
4. Warm tortillas in a dry skillet or on the grill.
5. Flake cooked fish into bite-sized pieces.
6. Assemble tacos: place fish on each tortilla, top with shredded cabbage, cilantro, and red onion.
7. Serve with lime wedges on the side.

Nutritional Information: 320 calories, 25g protein, 30g carbohydrates, 12g fat, 4g fiber, 55mg cholesterol, 280mg sodium, 500mg potassium.

Note: Nutritional values are estimated based on the ingredients and serving size. Actual values may vary slightly. The final presentation of your recipe may vary slightly from the image illustration.

Stuffed Peppers with Ground Turkey and Quinoa

Yield: 4 servings | **Prep time:** 20 minutes | **Cook time:** 40 minutes

Ingredients:
- 4 large bell peppers, tops cut off and seeds removed
- 1 lb ground turkey
- 1 cup cooked quinoa
- 1 small onion, finely chopped
- 2 cloves garlic, minced
- 1 can (14.5 oz) diced tomatoes, drained
- 1 teaspoon dried oregano
- 1 teaspoon dried basil
- 1/2 teaspoon salt
- 1/4 teaspoon black pepper
- 1 cup shredded mozzarella cheese
- 2 tablespoons olive oil

Directions:
1. Preheat oven to 375°F (190°C).
2. In a large skillet, heat olive oil over medium heat. Add onion and garlic, cooking until softened, about 5 minutes.
3. Add ground turkey to the skillet, cooking until browned and fully cooked.
4. Stir in cooked quinoa, diced tomatoes, oregano, basil, salt, and pepper. Cook for another 5 minutes, mixing well.
5. Spoon the turkey and quinoa mixture into the hollowed bell peppers, packing them tightly.
6. Place stuffed peppers in a baking dish, cover with foil, and bake for 30 minutes.
7. Remove foil, sprinkle mozzarella cheese on top, and bake for an additional 10 minutes, or until cheese is melted and bubbly.

Nutritional Information: 340 calories, 28g protein, 28g carbohydrates, 14g fat, 5g fiber, 65mg cholesterol, 520mg sodium, 700mg potassium.

Note: Nutritional values are estimated based on the ingredients and serving size. Actual values may vary slightly. The final presentation of your recipe may vary slightly from the image illustration.

Tilapia with Tomato Basil Relish

Yield: 4 servings | **Prep time:** 10 minutes | **Cook time:** 20 minutes

Ingredients:
- 4 tilapia fillets
- 2 tablespoons olive oil
- 1 pint cherry tomatoes, halved
- 1/4 cup fresh basil leaves, chopped
- 2 cloves garlic, minced
- 1 tablespoon balsamic vinegar
- Salt and pepper to taste
- Lemon wedges, for serving

Directions:
1. Preheat oven to 375°F (190°C).

2. Place tilapia fillets on a baking sheet and brush with 1 tablespoon of olive oil. Season with salt and pepper.

3. Bake tilapia for 15-20 minutes, or until fish is opaque and flakes easily with a fork.

4. Meanwhile, in a medium bowl, combine cherry tomatoes, basil, garlic, remaining olive oil, balsamic vinegar, salt, and pepper.

5. Once tilapia is done, top each fillet with the tomato basil relish.

6. Serve immediately with lemon wedges on the side.

Nutritional Information: 240 calories, 28g protein, 6g carbohydrates, 12g fat, 2g fiber, 65mg cholesterol, 180mg sodium, 750mg potassium.

Note: *Nutritional values are estimated based on the ingredients and serving size. Actual values may vary slightly. The final presentation of your recipe may vary slightly from the image illustration.*

Turkey Meatballs with Zucchini Noodles

Yield: 4 servings | **Prep time:** 20 minutes | **Cook time:** 25 minutes

Ingredients:
- 1 pound ground turkey
- 1/4 cup grated Parmesan cheese
- 1/4 cup breadcrumbs
- 1 large egg
- 2 cloves garlic, minced
- 1 teaspoon dried oregano
- Salt and pepper to taste
- 2 tablespoons olive oil
- 4 medium zucchinis, spiralized into noodles
- 1 cup marinara sauce
- Fresh basil leaves, for garnish

Directions:
1. Preheat oven to 400°F (200°C).

2. In a large bowl, combine ground turkey, Parmesan cheese, breadcrumbs, egg, garlic, oregano, salt, and pepper. Mix well and form into small meatballs.

3. Heat olive oil in a large skillet over medium-high heat. Add meatballs and cook until browned on all sides, about 5 minutes.

4. Transfer browned meatballs to a baking sheet and bake in the preheated oven for 15-20 minutes, until fully cooked.

5. In the same skillet, add spiralized zucchini noodles and cook for 2-3 minutes until just tender.

6. Heat marinara sauce in a small saucepan over medium heat until warm.

7. Serve meatballs over zucchini noodles, topped with marinara sauce and garnished with fresh basil leaves.

Nutritional Information: 310 calories, 25g protein, 14g carbohydrates, 18g fat, 4g fiber, 90mg cholesterol, 560mg sodium, 880mg potassium.

Note: *Nutritional values are estimated based on the ingredients and serving size. Actual values may vary slightly. The final presentation of your recipe may vary slightly from the image illustration.*

Mediterranean Veggie Pita

Yield: 4 servings | **Prep time:** 15 minutes | **Cook time:** 0 minutes

Ingredients:
- 4 whole wheat pita breads
- 1 cup hummus
- 1 cup cherry tomatoes, halved
- 1 cucumber, diced
- 1/2 red onion, thinly sliced
- 1/2 cup Kalamata olives, pitted and sliced
- 1/4 cup crumbled feta cheese
- 1/4 cup fresh parsley, chopped
- 2 tablespoons extra-virgin olive oil
- 1 tablespoon fresh lemon juice
- Salt and pepper to taste

Directions:
1. Cut each whole wheat pita bread in half to form pockets.
2. Spread a generous layer of hummus inside each pita pocket.
3. In a large bowl, combine the cherry tomatoes, diced cucumber, thinly sliced red onion, Kalamata olives, crumbled feta cheese, and chopped fresh parsley.
4. In a small bowl, whisk together the extra-virgin olive oil, fresh lemon juice, salt, and pepper.
5. Pour the dressing over the vegetable mixture and toss gently to combine.
6. Stuff each pita pocket with the dressed vegetable mixture.
7. Serve immediately and enjoy!

Nutritional Information: 300 calories, 8g protein, 35g carbohydrates, 14g fat, 6g fiber, 15mg cholesterol, 600mg sodium, 350mg potassium.

Note: *Nutritional values are estimated based on the ingredients and serving size. Actual values may vary slightly. The final presentation of your recipe may vary slightly from the image illustration.*

Grilled Chicken and Hummus Wrap

Yield: 4 servings | **Prep time:** 20 minutes | **Cook time:** 10 minutes

Ingredients:
- 2 boneless, skinless chicken breasts
- 1 tablespoon olive oil
- Salt and pepper to taste
- 4 whole wheat tortillas
- 1 cup hummus
- 1 cup mixed greens (such as arugula, spinach, and romaine)
- 1/2 cup cherry tomatoes, halved
- 1/2 cucumber, sliced
- 1/4 red onion, thinly sliced
- 1/4 cup crumbled feta cheese

Directions:
1. Preheat the grill to medium-high heat. Brush the chicken breasts with olive oil and season with salt and pepper.
2. Grill the chicken breasts for 5-6 minutes on each side, or until fully cooked and no longer pink inside. Remove from the grill and let rest for a few minutes before slicing into thin strips.
3. Lay out the whole wheat tortillas on a flat surface. Spread a generous layer of hummus onto each tortilla.
4. Arrange the mixed greens, halved cherry tomatoes, sliced cucumber, and thinly sliced red onion evenly on top of the hummus.
5. Add the grilled chicken strips and sprinkle with crumbled feta cheese.
6. Roll up the tortillas tightly, tucking in the sides as you go, to form wraps.
7. Serve immediately and enjoy!

Nutritional Information: 400 calories, 30g protein, 35g carbohydrates, 16g fat, 7g fiber, 70mg cholesterol, 650mg sodium, 450mg potassium.

Note: *Nutritional values are estimated based on the ingredients and serving size. Actual values may vary slightly. The final presentation of your recipe may vary slightly from the image illustration.*

Falafel Wrap with Tzatziki

Yield: 4 servings | **Prep time:** 20 minutes | **Cook time:** 15 minutes

Ingredients:
- 1 package (12 oz) frozen falafel, heated according to package instructions
- 4 large whole wheat tortillas
- 1 cup tzatziki sauce
- 1 cup cherry tomatoes, halved
- 1 cucumber, thinly sliced
- 1/4 red onion, thinly sliced
- 1/4 cup fresh parsley, chopped
- 1/4 cup crumbled feta cheese

Directions:
1. Heat the falafel according to the package instructions and set aside.
2. Lay out the whole wheat tortillas on a flat surface. Spread 1/4 cup of tzatziki sauce onto each tortilla.
3. Divide the heated falafel evenly among the tortillas, placing them in the center of each.
4. Top the falafel with halved cherry tomatoes, thinly sliced cucumber, thinly sliced red onion, chopped fresh parsley, and crumbled feta cheese.
5. Fold the sides of the tortillas over the filling and then roll them up tightly to form wraps.
6. Cut each wrap in half and serve immediately.

Nutritional Information: 350 calories, 12g protein, 45g carbohydrates, 12g fat, 8g fiber, 15mg cholesterol, 650mg sodium, 400mg potassium.

Note: *Nutritional values are estimated based on the ingredients and serving size. Actual values may vary slightly. The final presentation of your recipe may vary slightly from the image illustration.*

Roast Beef and Arugula Wrap

Yield: 4 servings | **Prep time:** 15 minutes | **Cook time:** 0 minutes

Ingredients:
- 4 large whole wheat tortillas
- 8 ounces thinly sliced roast beef
- 2 cups fresh arugula
- 1/2 cup roasted red peppers, sliced
- 1/4 red onion, thinly sliced
- 1/4 cup crumbled blue cheese
- 1/4 cup mayonnaise
- 1 tablespoon horseradish sauce
- Salt and pepper to taste

Directions:
1. Lay out the whole wheat tortillas on a flat surface.
2. In a small bowl, mix the mayonnaise and horseradish sauce until well combined.
3. Spread the mayonnaise mixture evenly on each tortilla.
4. Layer the roast beef slices, fresh arugula, roasted red peppers, thinly sliced red onion, and crumbled blue cheese evenly on each tortilla. Season with salt and pepper to taste.
5. Fold the sides of the tortillas over the filling and then roll them up tightly to form wraps.
6. Cut each wrap in half and serve immediately.

Nutritional Information: 350 calories, 20g protein, 30g carbohydrates, 18g fat, 4g fiber, 50mg cholesterol, 700mg sodium, 450mg potassium.

Note: *Nutritional values are estimated based on the ingredients and serving size. Actual values may vary slightly. The final presentation of your recipe may vary slightly from the image illustration.*

Lentil Soup with Spinach and Lemon

Yield: 4 servings | **Prep time:** 15 minutes | **Cook time:** 30 minutes

Ingredients:

- 1 cup green or brown lentils, rinsed
- 1 tablespoon olive oil
- 1 onion, chopped
- 2 carrots, chopped
- 2 celery stalks, chopped
- 3 cloves garlic, minced
- 6 cups vegetable broth
- 1 teaspoon ground cumin
- 1 teaspoon ground coriander
- 1/2 teaspoon turmeric
- 1/4 teaspoon cayenne pepper (optional)
- 4 cups fresh spinach, roughly chopped
- 1 lemon, juiced
- Salt and pepper to taste

Directions:

1. In a large pot, heat the olive oil over medium heat. Add the chopped onion, carrots, and celery, and cook until the vegetables are softened, about 5 minutes.

2. Stir in the minced garlic, ground cumin, ground coriander, turmeric, and cayenne pepper (if using), and cook for another 1-2 minutes until fragrant.

3. Add the rinsed lentils and vegetable broth to the pot. Bring to a boil, then reduce the heat and simmer for 20-25 minutes, or until the lentils are tender.

4. Stir in the chopped fresh spinach and cook until wilted, about 2-3 minutes.

5. Add the lemon juice and season with salt and pepper to taste.

6. Serve hot, garnished with additional lemon wedges if desired.

Nutritional Information: 220 calories, 12g protein, 30g carbohydrates, 6g fat, 10g fiber, 0mg cholesterol, 400mg sodium, 600mg potassium.

Note: *Nutritional values are estimated based on the ingredients and serving size. Actual values may vary slightly. The final presentation of your recipe may vary slightly from the image illustration.*

Tomato Basil Soup

Yield: 4 servings | **Prep time:** 10 minutes | **Cook time:** 25 minutes

Ingredients:

- 2 tablespoons olive oil
- 1 onion, chopped
- 2 cloves garlic, minced
- 2 cans (28 oz each) whole peeled tomatoes
- 2 cups vegetable broth
- 1 teaspoon sugar
- 1/2 teaspoon salt
- 1/4 teaspoon black pepper
- 1/4 cup fresh basil leaves, chopped
- 1/2 cup heavy cream (optional)

Directions:

1. In a large pot, heat the olive oil over medium heat. Add the chopped onion and cook until softened, about 5 minutes.

2. Add the minced garlic and cook for another 1-2 minutes until fragrant.

3. Stir in the whole peeled tomatoes (with their juice), vegetable broth, sugar, salt, and black pepper. Bring to a boil, then reduce the heat and simmer for 20 minutes.

4. Use an immersion blender to puree the soup until smooth. Alternatively, you can carefully transfer the soup to a blender in batches and blend until smooth.

5. Stir in the chopped fresh basil leaves and the heavy cream, if using. Cook for another 2-3 minutes until heated through.

6. Taste and adjust seasoning with additional salt and pepper if needed.

7. Serve hot, garnished with additional basil leaves if desired.

Nutritional Information: 180 calories, 3g protein, 15g carbohydrates, 12g fat, 4g fiber, 20mg cholesterol, 400mg sodium, 500mg potassium.

Note: *Nutritional values are estimated based on the ingredients and serving size. Actual values may vary slightly. The final presentation of your recipe may vary slightly from the image illustration.*

Chicken and Orzo Soup

Yield: 4 servings | **Prep time:** 15 minutes | **Cook time:** 25 minutes

Ingredients:

- 1 tablespoon olive oil
- 1 onion, chopped
- 2 carrots, chopped
- 2 celery stalks, chopped
- 2 cloves garlic, minced
- 6 cups chicken broth
- 1 cup cooked shredded chicken
- 3/4 cup orzo pasta
- 1 teaspoon dried thyme
- 1 bay leaf
- 1 cup baby spinach leaves
- Juice of 1 lemon
- Salt and pepper to taste

Directions:

1. In a large pot, heat the olive oil over medium heat. Add the chopped onion, carrots, and celery, and cook until the vegetables are softened, about 5 minutes.
2. Stir in the minced garlic and cook for another 1-2 minutes until fragrant.
3. Add the chicken broth, cooked shredded chicken, orzo pasta, dried thyme, and bay leaf. Bring to a boil, then reduce the heat and simmer for 15 minutes, or until the orzo is tender.
4. Stir in the baby spinach leaves and cook until wilted, about 2-3 minutes.
5. Add the lemon juice and season with salt and pepper to taste.
6. Remove the bay leaf before serving.
7. Serve hot.

Nutritional Information: 250 calories, 18g protein, 30g carbohydrates, 7g fat, 3g fiber, 50mg cholesterol, 700mg sodium, 400mg potassium.

Note: *Nutritional values are estimated based on the ingredients and serving size. Actual values may vary slightly. The final presentation of your recipe may vary slightly from the image illustration.*

Vegetable Minestrone

Yield: 4 servings | **Prep time:** 20 minutes | **Cook time:** 30 minutes

Ingredients:

- 2 tablespoons olive oil
- 1 onion, chopped
- 2 cloves garlic, minced
- 2 carrots, chopped
- 2 celery stalks, chopped
- 1 zucchini, diced
- 1 cup green beans, trimmed and cut into 1-inch pieces
- 1 can (15 oz) diced tomatoes
- 6 cups vegetable broth
- 1 can (15 oz) cannellini beans, drained and rinsed
- 1/2 cup small pasta shells or elbow macaroni
- 1 teaspoon dried oregano
- 1 teaspoon dried basil
- 1/4 teaspoon red pepper flakes (optional)
- 2 cups baby spinach leaves
- Salt and pepper to taste
- Grated Parmesan cheese for serving

Directions:

1. In a large pot, heat the olive oil over medium heat. Add the chopped onion, garlic, carrots, and celery, and cook until the vegetables are softened, about 5 minutes.
2. Stir in the diced zucchini and green beans, and cook for another 5 minutes.
3. Add the diced tomatoes, vegetable broth, cannellini beans, pasta, dried oregano, dried basil, and red pepper flakes (if using). Bring to a boil, then reduce the heat and simmer for 20 minutes, or until the pasta and vegetables are tender.
4. Stir in the baby spinach leaves and cook until wilted, about 2-3 minutes.
5. Season with salt and pepper to taste.
6. Serve hot, garnished with grated Parmesan cheese if desired.

Nutritional Information: 200 calories, 7g protein, 32g carbohydrates, 5g fat, 7g fiber, 0mg cholesterol, 600mg sodium, 500mg potassium.

Note: *Nutritional values are estimated based on the ingredients and serving size. Actual values may vary slightly. The final presentation of your recipe may vary slightly from the image illustration.*

Roasted Red Pepper and Tomato Soup

Yield: 4 servings | **Prep time:** 15 minutes | **Cook time:** 30 minutes

Ingredients:

- 4 large red bell peppers
- 2 tablespoons olive oil
- 1 onion, chopped
- 3 cloves garlic, minced
- 2 cans (28 oz each) whole peeled tomatoes
- 4 cups vegetable broth
- 1 teaspoon dried basil
- 1 teaspoon sugar
- Salt and pepper to taste
- 1/4 cup heavy cream (optional)

Directions:

1. Preheat your oven to 450°F (230°C). Place the red bell peppers on a baking sheet and roast for 20-25 minutes, turning occasionally, until the skins are charred and blistered.

2. Transfer the roasted peppers to a bowl, cover with plastic wrap, and let them steam for 10 minutes. Peel and seed the peppers, then chop them.

3. In a large pot, heat the olive oil over medium heat. Add the chopped onion and cook until softened, about 5 minutes.

4. Stir in the minced garlic and cook for another 1-2 minutes until fragrant.

5. Add the chopped roasted red peppers, whole peeled tomatoes (with their juice), vegetable broth, dried basil, and sugar. Bring to a boil, then reduce the heat and simmer for 15 minutes.

6. Use an immersion blender to puree the soup until smooth. Alternatively, you can carefully transfer the soup to a blender in batches and blend until smooth.

7. Stir in the heavy cream, if using, and season with salt and pepper to taste. Cook for another 2-3 minutes until heated through.

Nutritional Information: 180 calories, 3g protein, 20g carbohydrates, 10g fat, 4g fiber, 15mg cholesterol, 400mg sodium, 500mg potassium.

Note: *Nutritional values are estimated based on the ingredients and serving size. Actual values may vary slightly. The final presentation of your recipe may vary slightly from the image illustration.*

Greek Avgolemono Soup (Egg and Lemon Soup)

Yield: 4 servings | **Prep time:** 10 minutes | **Cook time:** 20 minutes

Ingredients:

- 6 cups chicken broth
- 1/2 cup orzo pasta
- 3 large eggs
- 1/4 cup fresh lemon juice (about 2 lemons)
- 2 cups cooked shredded chicken (optional)
- Salt and pepper to taste
- Fresh dill or parsley, chopped, for garnish

Directions:

1. In a large pot, bring the chicken broth to a boil over medium-high heat.

2. Add the orzo pasta and cook until tender, about 10 minutes.

3. While the orzo is cooking, whisk the eggs and lemon juice together in a medium bowl until frothy.

4. Once the orzo is cooked, reduce the heat to low. Gradually ladle about 1 cup of hot broth into the egg mixture, whisking constantly to temper the eggs.

5. Slowly pour the tempered egg mixture back into the pot, stirring constantly to prevent curdling.

6. Add the cooked shredded chicken, if using, and heat through, about 2-3 minutes. Do not let the soup boil.

7. Season with salt and pepper to taste. Serve hot, garnished with fresh dill or parsley.

Nutritional Information: 180 calories, 15g protein, 14g carbohydrates, 7g fat, 1g fiber, 130mg cholesterol, 800mg sodium, 300mg potassium.

Note: *Nutritional values are estimated based on the ingredients and serving size. Actual values may vary slightly. The final presentation of your recipe may vary slightly from the image illustration.*

Eggplant Parmesan

Yield: 4 servings | **Prep time:** 20 minutes | **Cook time:** 50 minutes

Ingredients:

- 2 large eggplants, sliced into 1/2-inch rounds
- 1 tablespoon salt
- 2 cups breadcrumbs
- 1 cup grated Parmesan cheese
- 2 teaspoons dried oregano
- 1 teaspoon dried basil
- 1/2 teaspoon garlic powder
- 1/2 teaspoon salt
- 1/4 teaspoon black pepper
- 3 large eggs
- 1/4 cup milk
- 2 cups marinara sauce
- 2 cups shredded mozzarella cheese
- 1/4 cup chopped fresh basil

Directions:

1. Preheat the oven to 375°F (190°C). Arrange the eggplant slices on a baking sheet and sprinkle with 1 tablespoon of salt. Let sit for 20 minutes, then rinse and pat dry.

2. In a shallow bowl, combine breadcrumbs, Parmesan cheese, oregano, basil, garlic powder, 1/2 teaspoon salt, and black pepper. In another bowl, whisk together the eggs and milk.

3. Dip each eggplant slice into the egg mixture, then coat with the breadcrumb mixture. Place the coated slices on a baking sheet lined with parchment paper.

4. Bake the eggplant slices for 25 minutes, flipping halfway through, until golden and crisp.

5. In a 9x13-inch baking dish, spread a thin layer of marinara sauce. Arrange a layer of eggplant slices over the sauce, then top with more sauce and a sprinkle of mozzarella. Repeat layers, ending with mozzarella on top.

6. Bake for 25 minutes, or until the cheese is melted and bubbly.

7. Garnish with chopped fresh basil before serving.

Nutritional Information: 400 calories, 18g protein, 45g carbohydrates, 18g fat, 6g fiber, 90mg cholesterol, 1050mg sodium, 700mg potassium.

Note: *Nutritional values are estimated based on the ingredients and serving size. Actual values may vary slightly. The final presentation of your recipe may vary slightly from the image illustration.*

Chicken and Broccoli Casserole

Yield: 4 servings | **Prep time:** 15 minutes | **Cook time:** 35 minutes

Ingredients:

- 2 cups cooked chicken, shredded
- 4 cups broccoli florets
- 1 cup cooked rice
- 1 can (10.5 oz) condensed cream of chicken soup
- 1/2 cup mayonnaise
- 1/2 cup shredded cheddar cheese
- 1/4 cup grated Parmesan cheese
- 1/4 cup milk
- 1 teaspoon garlic powder
- 1/2 teaspoon salt
- 1/4 teaspoon black pepper
- 1/4 cup breadcrumbs
- 2 tablespoons melted butter

Directions:

1. Preheat oven to 350°F (175°C).

2. In a large bowl, combine the shredded chicken, broccoli florets, and cooked rice.

3. In another bowl, mix the cream of chicken soup, mayonnaise, cheddar cheese, Parmesan cheese, milk, garlic powder, salt, and black pepper until well blended.

4. Pour the soup mixture over the chicken, broccoli, and rice, and stir until everything is evenly coated.

5. Transfer the mixture to a 9x13-inch baking dish, spreading it out evenly.

6. In a small bowl, mix the breadcrumbs with the melted butter, then sprinkle evenly over the top of the casserole.

7. Bake for 35 minutes, or until the casserole is bubbly and the topping is golden brown.

Nutritional Information: 450 calories, 30g protein, 28g carbohydrates, 24g fat, 3g fiber, 70mg cholesterol, 800mg sodium, 500mg potassium.

Note: *Nutritional values are estimated based on the ingredients and serving size. Actual values may vary slightly. The final presentation of your recipe may vary slightly from the image illustration.*

Shepherd's Pie

Yield: 4 servings | **Prep time:** 20 minutes | **Cook time:** 45 minutes

Ingredients:

- 1 pound ground beef or lamb
- 1 onion, finely chopped
- 2 cloves garlic, minced
- 1 cup frozen peas and carrots
- 1 cup beef broth
- 2 tablespoons tomato paste
- 1 tablespoon Worcestershire sauce

- 2 tablespoons all-purpose flour
- 1/2 teaspoon dried thyme
- 1/2 teaspoon salt
- 1/4 teaspoon black pepper
- 4 cups mashed potatoes
- 1/2 cup shredded cheddar cheese

Directions:

1. Preheat oven to 375°F (190°C).

2. In a large skillet, cook the ground beef or lamb over medium heat until browned, about 5-7 minutes. Drain any excess fat.

3. Add the chopped onion and minced garlic to the skillet and cook until softened, about 3-5 minutes.

4. Stir in the peas and carrots, beef broth, tomato paste, Worcestershire sauce, flour, dried thyme, salt, and black pepper. Cook, stirring frequently, until the mixture thickens, about 5 minutes.

5. Transfer the meat mixture to a 9x13-inch baking dish, spreading it out evenly.

6. Spread the mashed potatoes over the meat mixture, then sprinkle the shredded cheddar cheese on top.

7. Bake in the preheated oven for 20-25 minutes, or until the cheese is melted and the edges are bubbly.

Nutritional Information: 450 calories, 20g protein, 35g carbohydrates, 25g fat, 4g fiber, 70mg cholesterol, 800mg sodium, 600mg potassium.

Note: Nutritional values are estimated based on the ingredients and serving size. Actual values may vary slightly. The final presentation of your recipe may vary slightly from the image illustration.

Vegetable Lasagna

Yield: 4 servings | **Prep time:** 25 minutes | **Cook time:** 45 minutes

Ingredients:

- 9 lasagna noodles
- 2 cups ricotta cheese
- 2 cups shredded mozzarella cheese
- 1 cup grated Parmesan cheese
- 1 jar (24 ounces) marinara sauce
- 2 cups spinach, chopped
- 1 medium zucchini, thinly sliced
- 1 medium yellow squash, thinly sliced

- 1 cup mushrooms, sliced
- 1 small onion, chopped
- 2 cloves garlic, minced
- 2 tablespoons olive oil
- 1 teaspoon dried basil
- 1 teaspoon dried oregano
- Salt and pepper to taste

Directions:

1. Preheat oven to 375°F (190°C). Cook lasagna noodles according to package directions. Drain and set aside.

2. In a large skillet, heat olive oil over medium heat. Add onion and garlic, cook until softened. Add zucchini, yellow squash, and mushrooms, cooking until tender. Stir in spinach, basil, oregano, salt, and pepper.

3. Spread 1 cup of marinara sauce in the bottom of a 9x13-inch baking dish. Place 3 lasagna noodles over the sauce. Spread 1/3 of the ricotta cheese over the noodles, followed by 1/3 of the vegetable mixture, 1/3 of the mozzarella cheese, and 1/3 of the Parmesan cheese. Repeat layers two more times, ending with a layer of sauce and cheese.

4. Cover with aluminum foil and bake for 30 minutes. Remove foil and bake for an additional 15 minutes, or until bubbly and golden.

5. Let stand for 10 minutes before serving.

Nutritional Information: 480 calories, 22g protein, 55g carbohydrates, 20g fat, 6g fiber, 50mg cholesterol, 860mg sodium, 500mg potassium.

Note: Nutritional values are estimated based on the ingredients and serving size. Actual values may vary slightly. The final presentation of your recipe may vary slightly from the image illustration.

Grilled Salmon with Lemon and Dill

Yield: 4 servings | **Prep time:** 10 minutes | **Cook time:** 15 minutes

Ingredients:
- 4 salmon fillets (6 ounces each)
- 2 tablespoons olive oil
- 2 lemons, sliced
- 1 tablespoon fresh dill, chopped
- Salt and pepper to taste
- 1 tablespoon lemon juice

Directions:
1. Preheat the grill to medium-high heat.
2. Brush the salmon fillets with olive oil and season with salt and pepper.
3. Place lemon slices on the grill and cook for 1-2 minutes per side until slightly charred.
4. Place the salmon fillets on the grill, skin side down. Grill for 5-7 minutes per side until the salmon is cooked through and flakes easily with a fork.
5. In the last 2 minutes of grilling, squeeze lemon juice over the salmon fillets.
6. Remove from the grill and sprinkle with fresh dill.
7. Serve the grilled salmon with the charred lemon slices.

Nutritional Information: 350 calories, 34g protein, 0g carbohydrates, 23g fat, 1g fiber, 90mg cholesterol, 100mg sodium, 780mg potassium.

Note: *Nutritional values are estimated based on the ingredients and serving size. Actual values may vary slightly. The final presentation of your recipe may vary slightly from the image illustration.*

Baked Cod with Tomatoes and Olives

Yield: 4 servings | **Prep time:** 10 minutes | **Cook time:** 20 minutes

Ingredients:
- 1 1/2 pounds cod fillets
- 1 pint cherry tomatoes, halved
- 1/2 cup Kalamata olives, pitted and halved
- 3 cloves garlic, minced
- 2 tablespoons olive oil
- 1 tablespoon fresh lemon juice
- 1 teaspoon dried oregano
- Salt and pepper to taste
- 1/4 cup fresh parsley, chopped

Directions:
1. Preheat the oven to 400°F (200°C).
2. Place the cod fillets in a baking dish. Season with salt and pepper.
3. In a bowl, combine cherry tomatoes, olives, garlic, olive oil, lemon juice, and oregano. Mix well.
4. Spread the tomato and olive mixture over the cod fillets.
5. Bake in the preheated oven for 20 minutes, or until the cod is cooked through and flakes easily with a fork.
6. Sprinkle with chopped parsley before serving.
7. Serve hot with a side of your choice.

Nutritional Information: 220 calories, 30g protein, 6g carbohydrates, 10g fat, 2g fiber, 70mg cholesterol, 550mg sodium, 500mg potassium.

Note: *Nutritional values are estimated based on the ingredients and serving size. Actual values may vary slightly. The final presentation of your recipe may vary slightly from the image illustration.*

Seared Scallops with Lemon Butter Sauce

Yield: 4 servings | **Prep time:** 10 minutes | **Cook time:** 10 minutes

Ingredients:

- 1 1/2 pounds large sea scallops
- Salt and pepper to taste
- 2 tablespoons olive oil
- 1/4 cup dry white wine
- 1/4 cup fresh lemon juice
- 4 tablespoons unsalted butter, cut into pieces
- 2 cloves garlic, minced
- 2 tablespoons fresh parsley, chopped
- Lemon wedges, for garnish

Directions:

1. Pat the scallops dry with paper towels and season with salt and pepper.
2. Heat olive oil in a large skillet over medium-high heat.
3. Add the scallops to the skillet and sear for 2-3 minutes per side, until golden brown and opaque in the center. Remove from the skillet and set aside.
4. In the same skillet, add garlic and sauté for about 30 seconds until fragrant.
5. Add the white wine and lemon juice, and bring to a simmer. Cook for about 2 minutes until slightly reduced.
6. Reduce heat to low and whisk in the butter, one piece at a time, until the sauce is smooth and creamy.
7. Return the scallops to the skillet and spoon the sauce over them. Cook for an additional minute to heat through. Garnish with chopped parsley and serve with lemon wedges.

Nutritional Information: 320 calories, 28g protein, 5g carbohydrates, 20g fat, 1g fiber, 85mg cholesterol, 460mg sodium, 450mg potassium.

Note: *Nutritional values are estimated based on the ingredients and serving size. Actual values may vary slightly. The final presentation of your recipe may vary slightly from the image illustration.*

Fish Stew with Saffron and Potatoes

Yield: 4 servings | **Prep time:** 15 minutes | **Cook time:** 30 minutes

Ingredients:

- 1 1/2 pounds firm white fish fillets (such as cod or halibut), cut into chunks
- 1 tablespoon olive oil
- 1 large onion, diced
- 2 cloves garlic, minced
- 1/2 teaspoon saffron threads
- 4 cups fish stock or chicken broth
- 1 pound potatoes, peeled and cut into chunks
- 1 large tomato, diced
- 1/2 cup dry white wine
- Salt and pepper to taste
- 2 tablespoons fresh parsley, chopped
- Lemon wedges, for garnish

Directions:

1. Heat olive oil in a large pot over medium heat. Add the onion and cook until softened, about 5 minutes.
2. Add the garlic and saffron, and cook for another minute until fragrant.
3. Pour in the fish stock and white wine, then add the potatoes. Bring to a simmer and cook until the potatoes are tender, about 15 minutes.
4. Add the tomato and season with salt and pepper. Simmer for an additional 5 minutes.
5. Gently stir in the fish chunks and cook until the fish is opaque and cooked through, about 5-7 minutes.
6. Remove from heat and sprinkle with chopped parsley.
7. Serve hot, garnished with lemon wedges.

Nutritional Information: 320 calories, 30g protein, 25g carbohydrates, 10g fat, 3g fiber, 60mg cholesterol, 480mg sodium, 700mg potassium.

Note: *Nutritional values are estimated based on the ingredients and serving size. Actual values may vary slightly. The final presentation of your recipe may vary slightly from the image illustration.*

Mussels in White Wine Sauce

Yield: 4 servings | **Prep time:** 15 minutes | **Cook time:** 15 minutes

Ingredients:
- 2 pounds fresh mussels, scrubbed and debearded
- 2 tablespoons olive oil
- 4 cloves garlic, minced
- 1 shallot, finely chopped
- 1 cup dry white wine
- 1/2 cup chicken broth
- 2 tablespoons unsalted butter
- 1/4 teaspoon crushed red pepper flakes (optional)
- Salt and pepper to taste
- 1/4 cup fresh parsley, chopped
- Lemon wedges, for garnish

Directions:
1. Heat olive oil in a large pot over medium heat. Add the garlic and shallot, cooking until fragrant and translucent, about 3-4 minutes.

2. Pour in the white wine and chicken broth, then bring to a simmer.

3. Add the mussels to the pot, cover, and cook until the mussels open, about 5-7 minutes. Discard any mussels that do not open.

4. Stir in the butter and crushed red pepper flakes (if using), then season with salt and pepper to taste.

5. Remove from heat and sprinkle with fresh parsley.

6. Serve the mussels in bowls with the broth, garnished with lemon wedges.

Nutritional Information: 220 calories, 18g protein, 8g carbohydrates, 10g fat, 1g fiber, 50mg cholesterol, 620mg sodium, 450mg potassium.

Note: Nutritional values are estimated based on the ingredients and serving size. Actual values may vary slightly. The final presentation of your recipe may vary slightly from the image illustration.

Tuna Steaks with Avocado Salsa

Yield: 4 servings | **Prep time:** 15 minutes | **Cook time:** 10 minutes

Ingredients:
- 4 tuna steaks (6 oz each)
- 1 tablespoon olive oil
- Salt and pepper to taste
- 2 avocados, diced
- 1 small red onion, finely chopped
- 1 jalapeño, seeded and finely chopped
- 1/4 cup fresh cilantro, chopped
- 2 tablespoons lime juice
- 1 tablespoon olive oil (for salsa)
- Salt to taste

Directions:
1. Preheat a grill or grill pan over medium-high heat. Brush the tuna steaks with olive oil and season with salt and pepper.

2. Grill the tuna steaks for 2-3 minutes per side, or until desired doneness. Remove from grill and let rest.

3. In a medium bowl, combine the diced avocado, red onion, jalapeño, cilantro, lime juice, and olive oil. Season with salt to taste.

4. Serve the grilled tuna steaks topped with the avocado salsa.

Nutritional Information: 320 calories, 32g protein, 12g carbohydrates, 18g fat, 7g fiber, 55mg cholesterol, 300mg sodium, 700mg potassium.

Note: Nutritional values are estimated based on the ingredients and serving size. Actual values may vary slightly. The final presentation of your recipe may vary slightly from the image illustration.

Lamb Chops with Rosemary and Garlic

Yield: 4 servings | **Prep time:** 10 minutes | **Cook time:** 15 minutes

Ingredients:
- 8 lamb chops
- 2 tablespoons olive oil
- 4 cloves garlic, minced
- 2 tablespoons fresh rosemary, chopped
- Salt and pepper to taste
- 1 lemon, cut into wedges (for serving)

Directions:
1. Preheat the grill to medium-high heat.

2. In a small bowl, combine olive oil, minced garlic, and chopped rosemary.

3. Brush the lamb chops with the garlic and rosemary mixture, and season with salt and pepper.

4. Place the lamb chops on the grill and cook for 5-6 minutes per side, or until desired doneness is reached.

5. Remove from the grill and let rest for a few minutes.

6. Serve the lamb chops with lemon wedges on the side.

Nutritional Information: 400 calories, 35g protein, 1g carbohydrates, 28g fat, 0g fiber, 110mg cholesterol, 320mg sodium, 420mg potassium.

Note: *Nutritional values are estimated based on the ingredients and serving size. Actual values may vary slightly. The final presentation of your recipe may vary slightly from the image illustration.*

Chicken Marsala with Mushrooms

Yield: 4 servings | **Prep time:** 10 minutes | **Cook time:** 20 minutes

Ingredients:
- 4 boneless, skinless chicken breasts
- 1/2 cup all-purpose flour
- 1 teaspoon salt
- 1/2 teaspoon black pepper
- 2 tablespoons olive oil
- 8 ounces mushrooms, sliced
- 1/2 cup Marsala wine
- 1/2 cup chicken broth
- 2 tablespoons unsalted butter
- 2 tablespoons fresh parsley, chopped

Directions:
1. In a shallow dish, mix together flour, salt, and pepper. Dredge the chicken breasts in the flour mixture, shaking off any excess.

2. In a large skillet, heat olive oil over medium-high heat. Add the chicken breasts and cook until golden brown, about 5 minutes per side. Remove the chicken and set aside.

3. In the same skillet, add the mushrooms and cook until they are browned and tender, about 5 minutes.

4. Add Marsala wine and chicken broth to the skillet, stirring to scrape up any browned bits from the bottom. Bring to a simmer.

5. Return the chicken to the skillet and cook until the sauce has thickened and the chicken is cooked through, about 10 minutes.

6. Stir in the butter and sprinkle with fresh parsley before serving.

Nutritional Information: 400 calories, 35g protein, 10g carbohydrates, 20g fat, 1g fiber, 100mg cholesterol, 700mg sodium, 400mg potassium.

Note: *Nutritional values are estimated based on the ingredients and serving size. Actual values may vary slightly. The final presentation of your recipe may vary slightly from the image illustration.*

Beef Stroganoff with Sour Cream and Dill

Yield: 4 servings | **Prep time:** 15 minutes | **Cook time:** 30 minutes

Ingredients:
- 1 pound beef sirloin, thinly sliced
- 1 tablespoon olive oil
- 1 onion, finely chopped
- 2 cloves garlic, minced
- 8 ounces mushrooms, sliced
- 1/2 cup beef broth
- 1/2 cup sour cream
- 1 tablespoon Dijon mustard
- 1 teaspoon paprika
- 1 tablespoon fresh dill, chopped
- Salt and pepper to taste
- Cooked egg noodles for serving

Directions:
1. Heat olive oil in a large skillet over medium-high heat. Add beef slices and cook until browned, about 5 minutes. Remove the beef and set aside.

2. In the same skillet, add onions and garlic. Cook until softened, about 5 minutes.

3. Add mushrooms to the skillet and cook until they release their juices and start to brown, about 5 minutes.

4. Stir in beef broth, sour cream, Dijon mustard, and paprika. Bring the mixture to a simmer.

5. Return the beef to the skillet and cook until heated through, about 5 minutes. Season with salt and pepper to taste.

6. Sprinkle with fresh dill before serving.

7. Serve over cooked egg noodles.

Nutritional Information: 450 calories, 28g protein, 15g carbohydrates, 30g fat, 2g fiber, 120mg cholesterol, 600mg sodium, 500mg potassium.

Note: *Nutritional values are estimated based on the ingredients and serving size. Actual values may vary slightly. The final presentation of your recipe may vary slightly from the image illustration.*

Pork Tenderloin with Apple Cider Glaze

Yield: 4 servings | **Prep time:** 15 minutes | **Cook time:** 30 minutes

Ingredients:
- 1 pound pork tenderloin
- 1 tablespoon olive oil
- 1 cup apple cider
- 1/4 cup apple cider vinegar
- 2 tablespoons brown sugar
- 1 tablespoon Dijon mustard
- 2 cloves garlic, minced
- 1 teaspoon fresh thyme, chopped
- Salt and pepper to taste

Directions:
1. Preheat the oven to 375°F.

2. Season the pork tenderloin with salt and pepper. Heat olive oil in an oven-safe skillet over medium-high heat. Sear the pork on all sides until browned, about 5 minutes.

3. In a small bowl, mix together apple cider, apple cider vinegar, brown sugar, Dijon mustard, garlic, and thyme.

4. Pour the apple cider mixture over the pork in the skillet. Transfer the skillet to the preheated oven and roast for 20-25 minutes, or until the internal temperature reaches 145°F.

5. Remove the pork from the oven and transfer to a cutting board to rest for 5 minutes.

6. Place the skillet back on the stove over medium heat and simmer the sauce until it thickens, about 5 minutes.

7. Slice the pork tenderloin and drizzle with the apple cider glaze before serving.

Nutritional Information: 300 calories, 25g protein, 18g carbohydrates, 12g fat, 1g fiber, 75mg cholesterol, 350mg sodium, 450mg potassium.

Note: *Nutritional values are estimated based on the ingredients and serving size. Actual values may vary slightly. The final presentation of your recipe may vary slightly from the image illustration.*

Moroccan Spiced Chicken

Yield: 4 servings | **Prep time:** 15 minutes | **Cook time:** 30 minutes

Ingredients:
- 1.5 pounds boneless, skinless chicken thighs
- 1 tablespoon olive oil
- 2 teaspoons ground cumin
- 2 teaspoons ground coriander
- 1 teaspoon ground cinnamon
- 1 teaspoon ground ginger
- 1 teaspoon paprika
- 1/2 teaspoon ground turmeric
- 1/2 teaspoon cayenne pepper
- 2 cloves garlic, minced
- 1/2 cup chicken broth
- Salt and pepper to taste
- Fresh cilantro, chopped (for garnish)

Directions:
1. Preheat oven to 375°F.

2. In a small bowl, mix together cumin, coriander, cinnamon, ginger, paprika, turmeric, cayenne pepper, salt, and pepper.

3. Rub the spice mixture all over the chicken thighs.

4. Heat olive oil in a large oven-safe skillet over medium-high heat. Add the chicken thighs and sear on both sides until browned, about 5 minutes per side.

5. Add garlic to the skillet and cook for 1 minute until fragrant. Pour in the chicken broth.

6. Transfer the skillet to the preheated oven and bake for 20 minutes or until the chicken is cooked through.

7. Remove from oven and garnish with chopped fresh cilantro before serving.

Nutritional Information: 300 calories, 25g protein, 3g carbohydrates, 20g fat, 1g fiber, 100mg cholesterol, 450mg sodium, 400mg potassium.

Note: *Nutritional values are estimated based on the ingredients and serving size. Actual values may vary slightly. The final presentation of your recipe may vary slightly from the image illustration.*

Grilled Steak with Chimichurri Sauce

Yield: 4 servings | **Prep time:** 15 minutes | **Cook time:** 10 minutes

Ingredients:
- 1.5 pounds flank steak
- 1/2 cup olive oil
- 1/4 cup red wine vinegar
- 1/2 cup fresh parsley, chopped
- 1/4 cup fresh cilantro, chopped
- 4 cloves garlic, minced
- 1 teaspoon dried oregano
- 1/2 teaspoon red pepper flakes
- Salt and pepper to taste

Directions:
1. Preheat grill to high heat.

2. Season the flank steak with salt and pepper on both sides.

3. In a medium bowl, whisk together olive oil, red wine vinegar, parsley, cilantro, garlic, oregano, red pepper flakes, salt, and pepper to make the chimichurri sauce.

4. Grill the steak for about 4-5 minutes per side for medium-rare, or until desired doneness.

5. Remove the steak from the grill and let it rest for 5 minutes before slicing.

6. Slice the steak thinly against the grain.

7. Serve the sliced steak with the chimichurri sauce drizzled over the top.

Nutritional Information: 350 calories, 30g protein, 2g carbohydrates, 24g fat, 1g fiber, 90mg cholesterol, 200mg sodium, 500mg potassium.

Note: *Nutritional values are estimated based on the ingredients and serving size. Actual values may vary slightly. The final presentation of your recipe may vary slightly from the image illustration.*

Spaghetti with Pesto and Cherry Tomatoes

Yield: 4 servings | **Prep time:** 10 minutes | **Cook time:** 15 minutes

Ingredients:

- 12 ounces spaghetti
- 1/4 cup olive oil
- 2 cloves garlic, minced
- 1 pint cherry tomatoes, halved
- 1/2 cup prepared pesto
- Salt and pepper to taste
- 1/4 cup grated Parmesan cheese
- Fresh basil leaves, for garnish

Directions:

1. Cook the spaghetti according to the package instructions. Drain and set aside.

2. In a large skillet, heat the olive oil over medium heat. Add the minced garlic and sauté until fragrant, about 1 minute.

3. Add the halved cherry tomatoes to the skillet and cook until they start to soften, about 5 minutes.

4. Add the cooked spaghetti to the skillet and toss to combine with the tomatoes and garlic.

5. Stir in the pesto until the spaghetti is evenly coated. Season with salt and pepper to taste.

6. Sprinkle with grated Parmesan cheese and garnish with fresh basil leaves.

7. Serve immediately.

Nutritional Information: 400 calories, 12g protein, 56g carbohydrates, 14g fat, 4g fiber, 10mg cholesterol, 360mg sodium, 350mg potassium.

Note: *Nutritional values are estimated based on the ingredients and serving size. Actual values may vary slightly. The final presentation of your recipe may vary slightly from the image illustration.*

Risotto with Asparagus and Parmesan

Yield: 4 servings | **Prep time:** 15 minutes | **Cook time:** 25 minutes

Ingredients:

- 1 cup Arborio rice
- 1 tablespoon olive oil
- 1 small onion, finely chopped
- 2 cloves garlic, minced
- 1/2 cup dry white wine
- 4 cups chicken or vegetable broth, warmed
- 1 bunch asparagus, trimmed and cut into 1-inch pieces
- 1/2 cup grated Parmesan cheese
- 2 tablespoons butter
- Salt and pepper to taste
- Fresh parsley, chopped, for garnish

Directions:

1. In a large saucepan, heat the olive oil over medium heat. Add the chopped onion and garlic, sauté until translucent, about 3 minutes.

2. Add the Arborio rice to the pan and stir to coat with the oil. Cook for 2 minutes until the edges of the rice are translucent.

3. Pour in the white wine and cook, stirring constantly, until the wine is absorbed.

4. Begin adding the warmed broth, one ladle at a time, stirring frequently. Wait until the broth is almost completely absorbed before adding more.

5. After about 15 minutes, stir in the asparagus pieces. Continue adding broth and stirring until the rice is creamy and tender, about 5-7 more minutes.

6. Remove from heat and stir in the Parmesan cheese and butter. Season with salt and pepper to taste.

7. Garnish with chopped parsley and serve immediately.

Nutritional Information: 350 calories, 10g protein, 50g carbohydrates, 12g fat, 3g fiber, 20mg cholesterol, 750mg sodium, 300mg potassium.

Note: *Nutritional values are estimated based on the ingredients and serving size. Actual values may vary slightly. The final presentation of your recipe may vary slightly from the image illustration.*

Penne Arrabbiata

Yield: 4 servings | **Prep time:** 10 minutes | **Cook time:** 20 minutes

Ingredients:

- 12 oz penne pasta
- 2 tablespoons olive oil
- 4 cloves garlic, minced
- 1 teaspoon red pepper flakes (adjust to taste)
- 1 can (28 oz) crushed tomatoes
- 1 teaspoon salt
- 1/2 teaspoon black pepper
- 1 teaspoon sugar (optional, to balance acidity)
- 1/4 cup fresh basil, chopped
- Grated Parmesan cheese, for serving

Directions:

1. Cook the penne pasta according to package instructions. Drain and set aside.

2. In a large skillet, heat the olive oil over medium heat. Add the minced garlic and red pepper flakes, sauté for 1-2 minutes until fragrant.

3. Add the crushed tomatoes to the skillet, stirring to combine. Season with salt, black pepper, and sugar if using. Bring the sauce to a simmer.

4. Reduce the heat and let the sauce simmer for about 10-15 minutes, stirring occasionally, until it thickens.

5. Stir in the cooked penne pasta, ensuring it is well coated with the sauce.

6. Add the fresh basil and toss to combine. Adjust seasoning to taste.

7. Serve hot, topped with grated Parmesan cheese.

Nutritional Information: 400 calories, 12g protein, 70g carbohydrates, 10g fat, 5g fiber, 0mg cholesterol, 800mg sodium, 400mg potassium.

Note: Nutritional values are estimated based on the ingredients and serving size. Actual values may vary slightly. The final presentation of your recipe may vary slightly from the image illustration.

Fettuccine Alfredo with Shrimp

Yield: 4 servings | **Prep time:** 10 minutes | **Cook time:** 20 minutes

Ingredients:

- 12 oz fettuccine pasta
- 1 lb large shrimp, peeled and deveined
- 2 tablespoons olive oil
- 3 cloves garlic, minced
- 1 cup heavy cream
- 1 cup grated Parmesan cheese
- 4 tablespoons unsalted butter
- 1/2 teaspoon salt
- 1/4 teaspoon black pepper
- 1/4 cup fresh parsley, chopped (optional)

Directions:

1. Cook the fettuccine pasta according to package instructions. Drain and set aside.

2. In a large skillet, heat the olive oil over medium-high heat. Add the shrimp and cook for 2-3 minutes on each side until they are pink and opaque. Remove the shrimp from the skillet and set aside.

3. In the same skillet, add the minced garlic and sauté for 1-2 minutes until fragrant.

4. Add the heavy cream and butter to the skillet, stirring until the butter is melted and the mixture is smooth. Bring to a simmer.

5. Reduce the heat to low and stir in the grated Parmesan cheese until the sauce is creamy. Season with salt and black pepper.

6. Add the cooked fettuccine and shrimp to the skillet, tossing to coat evenly with the sauce.

7. Serve hot, garnished with chopped fresh parsley if desired.

Nutritional Information: 650 calories, 30g protein, 45g carbohydrates, 40g fat, 2g fiber, 220mg cholesterol, 750mg sodium, 350mg potassium.

Note: Nutritional values are estimated based on the ingredients and serving size. Actual values may vary slightly. The final presentation of your recipe may vary slightly from the image illustration.

Paella with Chicken and Seafood

Yield: 4 servings | **Prep time:** 15 minutes | **Cook time:** 40 minutes

Ingredients:

- 2 tablespoons olive oil
- 1/2 lb chicken thighs, boneless and skinless, cut into bite-sized pieces
- 1/2 lb large shrimp, peeled and deveined
- 1/2 lb mussels, cleaned
- 1/2 lb clams, cleaned
- 1 small onion, finely chopped
- 1 red bell pepper, diced
- 1 cup short-grain rice (such as Arborio)
- 1/2 teaspoon smoked paprika
- 1/4 teaspoon saffron threads
- 1/4 teaspoon black pepper
- 2 cloves garlic, minced
- 4 cups chicken broth
- 1 cup frozen peas
- 1 lemon, cut into wedges
- 2 tablespoons fresh parsley, chopped

Directions:

1. Heat olive oil in a large paella pan or skillet over medium heat. Brown the chicken pieces for 5-7 minutes, then set aside.

2. In the same pan, sauté the onion and red bell pepper until softened, about 5 minutes. Add garlic and cook for 1 minute.

3. Stir in the rice, smoked paprika, saffron threads, and black pepper, toasting the rice for 1-2 minutes.

4. Pour in chicken broth and bring to a simmer. Reduce heat to low and cook uncovered for 20 minutes, stirring occasionally.

5. Add the browned chicken, shrimp, mussels, clams, and peas. Cover and cook for 10 minutes, or until the seafood is cooked through and the rice is tender.

6. Remove from heat and let rest for 5 minutes. Garnish with parsley and lemon wedges before serving.

7. Serve hot, allowing each person to squeeze lemon juice over their portion.

Nutritional Information: 550 calories, 35g protein, 60g carbohydrates, 18g fat, 4g fiber, 120mg cholesterol, 900mg sodium, 500mg potassium.

Note: *Nutritional values are estimated based on the ingredients and serving size. Actual values may vary slightly. The final presentation of your recipe may vary slightly from the image illustration.*

Baked Ziti with Sausage and Peppers

Yield: 4 servings | **Prep time:** 15 minutes | **Cook time:** 45 minutes

Ingredients:

- 12 oz ziti pasta
- 1 tablespoon olive oil
- 1 lb Italian sausage, casings removed
- 1 red bell pepper, sliced
- 1 yellow bell pepper, sliced
- 1 small onion, chopped
- 2 cloves garlic, minced
- 2 cups marinara sauce
- 1 cup ricotta cheese
- 2 cups shredded mozzarella cheese
- 1/2 cup grated Parmesan cheese
- 1 teaspoon dried oregano
- 1 teaspoon dried basil
- Salt and pepper to taste

Directions:

1. Preheat the oven to 375°F (190°C). Cook the ziti pasta according to package directions, then drain and set aside.

2. In a large skillet, heat olive oil over medium heat. Add the sausage, breaking it up with a spoon, and cook until browned, about 5-7 minutes.

3. Add the bell peppers, onion, and garlic to the skillet. Cook until the vegetables are softened, about 5 minutes. Stir in the marinara sauce, oregano, basil, salt, and pepper. Simmer for 10 minutes.

4. In a large mixing bowl, combine the cooked pasta with the sausage and pepper mixture. Add the ricotta cheese and 1 cup of mozzarella, stirring until well combined.

5. Transfer the pasta mixture to a 9x13-inch baking dish. Top with the remaining 1 cup of mozzarella and the Parmesan cheese.

6. Cover the baking dish with aluminum foil and bake for 20 minutes. Remove the foil and bake for an additional 10-15 minutes, or until the cheese is melted and bubbly.

7. Let the baked ziti rest for 5 minutes before serving.

Nutritional Information: 550 calories, 26g protein, 60g carbohydrates, 25g fat, 4g fiber, 80mg cholesterol, 1000mg sodium, 600mg potassium.

Note: *Nutritional values are estimated based on the ingredients and serving size. Actual values may vary slightly. The final presentation of your recipe may vary slightly from the image illustration.*

Stuffed Zucchini Boats with Lentils and Rice

Yield: 4 servings | **Prep time:** 15 minutes | **Cook time:** 40 minutes

Ingredients:
- 4 medium zucchinis
- 1 cup cooked lentils
- 1 cup cooked rice
- 1 small onion, diced
- 2 cloves garlic, minced
- 1/2 cup diced tomatoes
- 1 teaspoon ground cumin
- 1 teaspoon ground coriander
- 1 tablespoon olive oil
- Salt and pepper to taste
- 1/4 cup grated Parmesan cheese (optional)
- Fresh parsley, chopped (for garnish)

Directions:
1. Preheat oven to 375°F (190°C).

2. Cut zucchinis in half lengthwise and scoop out the centers to create boats. Place them in a baking dish.

3. In a large skillet, heat olive oil over medium heat. Add onion and garlic, and sauté until softened, about 5 minutes.

4. Stir in cooked lentils, cooked rice, diced tomatoes, cumin, coriander, salt, and pepper. Cook for another 5 minutes until heated through.

5. Spoon the lentil and rice mixture into the zucchini boats, packing them tightly.

6. If using, sprinkle grated Parmesan cheese over the stuffed zucchinis.

7. Cover the baking dish with foil and bake for 25 minutes. Remove the foil and bake for an additional 10 minutes until zucchinis are tender and the tops are golden brown.

Nutritional Information: 210 calories, 8g protein, 34g carbohydrates, 6g fat, 6g fiber, 5mg cholesterol, 240mg sodium, 500mg potassium.

Note: Nutritional values are estimated based on the ingredients and serving size. Actual values may vary slightly. The final presentation of your recipe may vary slightly from the image illustration.

Vegetable Paella

Yield: 4 servings | **Prep time:** 15 minutes | **Cook time:** 45 minutes

Ingredients:
- 2 tablespoons olive oil
- 1 onion, finely chopped
- 3 cloves garlic, minced
- 1 red bell pepper, diced
- 1 yellow bell pepper, diced
- 1 cup green beans, trimmed and cut into 1-inch pieces
- 1 cup cherry tomatoes, halved
- 1 cup peas
- 1 1/2 cups Arborio rice
- 1/2 teaspoon saffron threads
- 1 teaspoon smoked paprika
- 4 cups vegetable broth
- Salt and pepper to taste
- 1 lemon, cut into wedges (for garnish)
- Fresh parsley, chopped (for garnish)

Directions:
1. Heat olive oil in a large paella pan or skillet over medium heat. Add onion and garlic, and sauté until softened, about 5 minutes.

2. Add red and yellow bell peppers, green beans, and cherry tomatoes. Cook for another 5 minutes until the vegetables begin to soften.

3. Stir in the Arborio rice, saffron threads, and smoked paprika. Cook for 2 minutes, stirring constantly to coat the rice with the spices.

4. Pour in the vegetable broth and bring to a boil. Reduce heat to low and simmer, uncovered, for 20-25 minutes, or until the rice is tender and the liquid is mostly absorbed.

5. Add peas and cook for an additional 5 minutes.

6. Season with salt and pepper to taste.

7. Garnish with lemon wedges and fresh parsley before serving.

Nutritional Information: 320 calories, 8g protein, 56g carbohydrates, 7g fat, 6g fiber, 0mg cholesterol, 580mg sodium, 450mg potassium.

Note: Nutritional values are estimated based on the ingredients and serving size. Actual values may vary slightly. The final presentation of your recipe may vary slightly from the image illustration.

Spinach and Ricotta Stuffed Peppers

Yield: 4 servings | **Prep time:** 20 minutes | **Cook time:** 30 minutes

Ingredients:

- 4 large bell peppers, halved and seeded
- 2 tablespoons olive oil
- 1 onion, finely chopped
- 3 cloves garlic, minced
- 10 ounces fresh spinach, chopped
- 1 cup ricotta cheese
- 1/2 cup grated Parmesan cheese
- 1 egg, beaten
- Salt and pepper to taste
- 1/4 teaspoon nutmeg
- 1/2 cup marinara sauce
- Fresh basil, chopped (for garnish)

Directions:

1. Preheat the oven to 375°F (190°C). Place the bell pepper halves in a baking dish.

2. Heat olive oil in a large skillet over medium heat. Add onion and garlic, sauté until softened, about 5 minutes.

3. Add the chopped spinach to the skillet and cook until wilted, about 3-4 minutes. Remove from heat and let cool slightly.

4. In a large bowl, combine the spinach mixture, ricotta cheese, Parmesan cheese, egg, nutmeg, salt, and pepper. Mix well.

5. Stuff each bell pepper half with the ricotta and spinach mixture. Top with a spoonful of marinara sauce.

6. Cover the baking dish with aluminum foil and bake for 25 minutes. Remove the foil and bake for an additional 5 minutes, or until the peppers are tender and the filling is heated through.

7. Garnish with chopped fresh basil before serving.

Nutritional Information: 240 calories, 12g protein, 18g carbohydrates, 14g fat, 4g fiber, 50mg cholesterol, 460mg sodium, 650mg potassium.

Note: Nutritional values are estimated based on the ingredients and serving size. Actual values may vary slightly. The final presentation of your recipe may vary slightly from the image illustration.

Butternut Squash and Chickpea Stew

Yield: 4 servings | **Prep time:** 15 minutes | **Cook time:** 45 minutes

Ingredients:

- 2 tablespoons olive oil
- 1 onion, finely chopped
- 3 cloves garlic, minced
- 1 medium butternut squash, peeled, seeded, and cubed
- 1 can (15 ounces) chickpeas, drained and rinsed
- 1 can (14.5 ounces) diced tomatoes
- 4 cups vegetable broth
- 1 teaspoon ground cumin
- 1 teaspoon ground coriander
- 1/2 teaspoon ground cinnamon
- Salt and pepper to taste
- 1/4 cup chopped fresh cilantro (optional, for garnish)

Directions:

1. Heat olive oil in a large pot over medium heat. Add the onion and garlic, and sauté until softened, about 5 minutes.

2. Add the cubed butternut squash to the pot and cook for an additional 5 minutes, stirring occasionally.

3. Stir in the chickpeas, diced tomatoes, vegetable broth, cumin, coriander, and cinnamon. Season with salt and pepper to taste.

4. Bring the stew to a boil, then reduce the heat and let it simmer, covered, for 30 minutes or until the butternut squash is tender.

5. Adjust the seasoning if necessary and simmer for another 5 minutes.

6. Serve hot, garnished with chopped fresh cilantro if desired.

Nutritional Information: 250 calories, 8g protein, 40g carbohydrates, 8g fat, 8g fiber, 0mg cholesterol, 600mg sodium, 700mg potassium.

Note: Nutritional values are estimated based on the ingredients and serving size. Actual values may vary slightly. The final presentation of your recipe may vary slightly from the image illustration.

Olive Oil and Lemon Cake

Yield: 6 servings | **Prep time:** 15 minutes | **Cook time:** 35 minutes

Ingredients:
- 1 1/2 cups all-purpose flour
- 1 teaspoon baking powder
- 1/2 teaspoon baking soda
- 1/4 teaspoon salt
- 3/4 cup granulated sugar
- 2 large eggs
- 1/2 cup extra virgin olive oil
- 1/2 cup whole milk
- 1/4 cup freshly squeezed lemon juice
- 1 tablespoon lemon zest
- 1 teaspoon vanilla extract

Directions:
1. Preheat the oven to 350°F (175°C) and grease a 9-inch round cake pan.
2. In a medium bowl, whisk together the flour, baking powder, baking soda, and salt.
3. In a large bowl, beat the sugar and eggs until light and fluffy. Gradually add the olive oil, continuing to beat until well combined.
4. Mix in the milk, lemon juice, lemon zest, and vanilla extract until smooth.
5. Gradually add the dry ingredients to the wet ingredients, mixing until just combined.
6. Pour the batter into the prepared cake pan and bake for 35 minutes, or until a toothpick inserted into the center comes out clean.
7. Allow the cake to cool in the pan for 10 minutes, then transfer to a wire rack to cool completely.

Nutritional Information: 290 calories, 4g protein, 34g carbohydrates, 15g fat, 1g fiber, 45mg cholesterol, 180mg sodium, 100mg potassium.

Note: *Nutritional values are estimated based on the ingredients and serving size. Actual values may vary slightly. The final presentation of your recipe may vary slightly from the image illustration.*

Almond Flour Biscotti

Yield: 6 servings | **Prep time:** 15 minutes | **Cook time:** 45 minutes

Ingredients:
- 2 cups almond flour
- 1/2 cup granulated sugar
- 1 teaspoon baking powder
- 1/4 teaspoon salt
- 2 large eggs
- 1 teaspoon vanilla extract
- 1/2 teaspoon almond extract
- 1/2 cup sliced almonds

Directions:
1. Preheat the oven to 325°F (165°C) and line a baking sheet with parchment paper.
2. In a medium bowl, whisk together the almond flour, sugar, baking powder, and salt.
3. In another bowl, beat the eggs, vanilla extract, and almond extract until well combined.
4. Gradually add the dry ingredients to the wet ingredients, mixing until a dough forms. Stir in the sliced almonds.
5. Shape the dough into a log about 12 inches long and 3 inches wide on the prepared baking sheet.
6. Bake for 25 minutes, then remove from the oven and let cool for 10 minutes. Reduce the oven temperature to 300°F (150°C).
7. Slice the log into 1/2-inch thick slices and place the slices cut-side down on the baking sheet. Bake for an additional 20 minutes, flipping the biscotti halfway through, until golden and crisp. Let cool completely on a wire rack.

Nutritional Information: 230 calories, 6g protein, 18g carbohydrates, 16g fat, 3g fiber, 35mg cholesterol, 70mg sodium, 150mg potassium.

Note: *Nutritional values are estimated based on the ingredients and serving size. Actual values may vary slightly. The final presentation of your recipe may vary slightly from the image illustration.*

Fig and Walnut Bread

Yield: 6 servings | **Prep time:** 15 minutes | **Cook time:** 55 minutes

Ingredients:

- 1 1/2 cups all-purpose flour
- 1/2 teaspoon baking powder
- 1/2 teaspoon baking soda
- 1/2 teaspoon salt
- 1/2 teaspoon ground cinnamon
- 1/4 teaspoon ground nutmeg
- 1/2 cup granulated sugar
- 1/2 cup packed brown sugar
- 2 large eggs
- 1/2 cup vegetable oil
- 1/2 cup plain Greek yogurt
- 1 teaspoon vanilla extract
- 1 cup dried figs, chopped
- 1/2 cup walnuts, chopped

Directions:

1. Preheat the oven to 350°F (175°C) and grease a 9x5-inch loaf pan.
2. In a medium bowl, whisk together the flour, baking powder, baking soda, salt, cinnamon, and nutmeg.
3. In a large bowl, beat the granulated sugar, brown sugar, and eggs until well combined. Add the oil, yogurt, and vanilla extract, and mix until smooth.
4. Gradually add the dry ingredients to the wet ingredients, mixing until just combined.
5. Fold in the chopped figs and walnuts.
6. Pour the batter into the prepared loaf pan and spread it evenly.
7. Bake for 50-55 minutes, or until a toothpick inserted into the center comes out clean. Let the bread cool in the pan for 10 minutes, then transfer to a wire rack to cool completely.

Nutritional Information: 320 calories, 5g protein, 46g carbohydrates, 13g fat, 3g fiber, 35mg cholesterol, 150mg sodium, 190mg potassium.

Note: *Nutritional values are estimated based on the ingredients and serving size. Actual values may vary slightly. The final presentation of your recipe may vary slightly from the image illustration.*

Banana Nut Muffins

Yield: 6 servings | **Prep time:** 15 minutes | **Cook time:** 25 minutes

Ingredients:

- 1 1/2 cups all-purpose flour
- 1 teaspoon baking soda
- 1/4 teaspoon salt
- 3 large ripe bananas, mashed
- 3/4 cup granulated sugar
- 1 large egg, beaten
- 1/3 cup unsalted butter, melted
- 1/2 cup chopped walnuts

Directions:

1. Preheat the oven to 350°F (175°C). Line a muffin tin with paper liners.
2. In a large bowl, combine the flour, baking soda, and salt.
3. In another bowl, mix the mashed bananas, sugar, egg, and melted butter.
4. Add the wet ingredients to the dry ingredients and mix until just combined. Fold in the chopped walnuts.
5. Spoon the batter into the prepared muffin tin, filling each cup about 2/3 full.
6. Bake for 20-25 minutes, or until a toothpick inserted into the center of a muffin comes out clean.
7. Let the muffins cool in the tin for 5 minutes before transferring to a wire rack to cool completely.

Nutritional Information: 220 calories, 4g protein, 30g carbohydrates, 10g fat, 2g fiber, 40mg cholesterol, 150mg sodium, 100mg potassium.

Note: *Nutritional values are estimated based on the ingredients and serving size. Actual values may vary slightly. The final presentation of your recipe may vary slightly from the image illustration.*

Frozen Yogurt with Berries

Yield: 4 servings | **Prep time:** 10 minutes | **Cook time:** 0 minutes

Ingredients:
- 2 cups plain Greek yogurt
- 1/4 cup honey
- 1 teaspoon vanilla extract
- 1 cup mixed berries (strawberries, blueberries, raspberries)

Directions:
1. In a medium bowl, mix the Greek yogurt, honey, and vanilla extract until well combined.
2. Gently fold in the mixed berries.
3. Transfer the mixture to an airtight container and spread it evenly.
4. Freeze for at least 2 hours, or until firm.
5. Scoop and serve immediately.

Nutritional Information: 150 calories, 8g protein, 25g carbohydrates, 2g fat, 3g fiber, 10mg cholesterol, 50mg sodium, 150mg potassium.

Note: *Nutritional values are estimated based on the ingredients and serving size. Actual values may vary slightly. The final presentation of your recipe may vary slightly from the image illustration.*

Mango Sorbet

Yield: 4 servings | **Prep time:** 10 minutes | **Cook time:** 0 minutes

Ingredients:
- 4 ripe mangoes, peeled and diced
- 1/4 cup lime juice
- 1/4 cup sugar
- 1/4 cup water

Directions:
1. In a blender, combine the mangoes, lime juice, sugar, and water.
2. Blend until smooth and the sugar is completely dissolved.
3. Pour the mixture into an airtight container and freeze for about 4 hours, stirring every hour to break up any ice crystals.
4. Once the sorbet is firm, scoop and serve immediately.

Nutritional Information: 150 calories, 1g protein, 38g carbohydrates, 0.5g fat, 3g fiber, 0mg cholesterol, 5mg sodium, 300mg potassium.

Note: *Nutritional values are estimated based on the ingredients and serving size. Actual values may vary slightly. The final presentation of your recipe may vary slightly from the image illustration.*

Watermelon Granita

Yield: 4 servings | **Prep time:** 10 minutes | **Cook time:** 0 minutes

Ingredients:
- 4 cups seedless watermelon, diced
- 1/4 cup sugar
- 2 tablespoons lime juice
- 1/4 cup water

Directions:
1. In a blender, combine the watermelon, sugar, lime juice, and water.

2. Blend until smooth.

3. Pour the mixture into a shallow baking dish and place in the freezer.

4. After 30 minutes, stir the mixture with a fork to break up any ice crystals.

5. Repeat this process every 30 minutes for about 2 hours, until the granita is fully frozen and fluffy.

6. Serve immediately, scooping into bowls with a fork.

Nutritional Information: 100 calories, 1g protein, 25g carbohydrates, 0g fat, 1g fiber, 0mg cholesterol, 2mg sodium, 270mg potassium.

Note: *Nutritional values are estimated based on the ingredients and serving size. Actual values may vary slightly. The final presentation of your recipe may vary slightly from the image illustration.*

Lemon and Mint Ice Cream

Yield: 4 servings | **Prep time:** 20 minutes | **Cook time:** 0 minutes

Ingredients:
- 2 cups heavy cream
- 1 cup whole milk
- 3/4 cup granulated sugar
- 1/2 cup freshly squeezed lemon juice
- 1 tablespoon lemon zest
- 1/4 cup fresh mint leaves, finely chopped
- 1 teaspoon vanilla extract

Directions:
1. In a large mixing bowl, combine the heavy cream, whole milk, and granulated sugar. Whisk until the sugar is fully dissolved.

2. Add the lemon juice, lemon zest, chopped mint leaves, and vanilla extract to the mixture. Stir until well blended.

3. Pour the mixture into an ice cream maker and churn according to the manufacturer's instructions until the ice cream is thick and creamy.

4. Transfer the ice cream to a lidded container and freeze for at least 4 hours or until firm.

5. Scoop and serve the ice cream garnished with extra mint leaves if desired.

Nutritional Information: 290 calories, 3g protein, 29g carbohydrates, 18g fat, 0g fiber, 70mg cholesterol, 40mg sodium, 100mg potassium.

Note: *Nutritional values are estimated based on the ingredients and serving size. Actual values may vary slightly. The final presentation of your recipe may vary slightly from the image illustration.*

Grilled Peaches with Honey and Almonds

Yield: 4 servings | **Prep time:** 10 minutes | **Cook time:** 10 minutes

Ingredients:
- 4 ripe peaches, halved and pitted
- 2 tablespoons olive oil
- 2 tablespoons honey
- 1/4 cup sliced almonds
- 1/2 teaspoon ground cinnamon (optional)
- Fresh mint leaves for garnish (optional)

Directions:
1. Preheat the grill to medium-high heat.

2. Brush the cut sides of the peach halves with olive oil.

3. Place the peaches cut side down on the grill and cook for 4-5 minutes, until grill marks appear and the peaches are slightly softened.

4. Flip the peaches and grill for an additional 2-3 minutes.

5. Remove the peaches from the grill and drizzle with honey.

6. Sprinkle sliced almonds over the peaches and, if desired, a pinch of ground cinnamon.

7. Garnish with fresh mint leaves and serve warm.

Nutritional Information: 150 calories, 2g protein, 20g carbohydrates, 7g fat, 3g fiber, 0mg cholesterol, 0mg sodium, 280mg potassium.

Note: *Nutritional values are estimated based on the ingredients and serving size. Actual values may vary slightly. The final presentation of your recipe may vary slightly from the image illustration.*

Apple and Cinnamon Compote

Yield: 4 servings | **Prep time:** 10 minutes | **Cook time:** 20 minutes

Ingredients:
- 4 large apples, peeled, cored, and diced
- 1/4 cup granulated sugar
- 1/2 teaspoon ground cinnamon
- 1/4 teaspoon ground nutmeg
- 1/4 cup water
- 1 teaspoon lemon juice

Directions:
1. In a medium saucepan, combine the diced apples, sugar, ground cinnamon, ground nutmeg, and water.

2. Bring the mixture to a boil over medium-high heat, then reduce the heat to low.

3. Simmer the apples for 15-20 minutes, stirring occasionally, until the apples are tender and the mixture has thickened.

4. Remove from heat and stir in the lemon juice.

5. Allow the compote to cool slightly before serving.

6. Serve warm or chilled, as desired.

Nutritional Information: 130 calories, 0g protein, 34g carbohydrates, 0g fat, 4g fiber, 0mg cholesterol, 0mg sodium, 220mg potassium.

Note: *Nutritional values are estimated based on the ingredients and serving size. Actual values may vary slightly. The final presentation of your recipe may vary slightly from the image illustration.*

Orange and Pomegranate Salad

Yield: 4 servings | **Prep time:** 15 minutes | **Cook time:** 0 minutes

Ingredients:

- 4 large oranges, peeled and segmented
- 1 cup pomegranate seeds
- 1 tablespoon honey
- 1 tablespoon fresh mint leaves, chopped
- 1 tablespoon lime juice

Directions:

1. In a large bowl, combine the orange segments and pomegranate seeds.

2. Drizzle the honey over the fruit and gently toss to coat.

3. Add the chopped mint leaves and lime juice to the bowl.

4. Gently toss the salad to combine all the ingredients.

5. Let the salad sit for 5 minutes to allow the flavors to meld.

6. Serve chilled or at room temperature.

Nutritional Information: 120 calories, 1g protein, 30g carbohydrates, 0g fat, 4g fiber, 0mg cholesterol, 2mg sodium, 250mg potassium.

Note: *Nutritional values are estimated based on the ingredients and serving size. Actual values may vary slightly. The final presentation of your recipe may vary slightly from the image illustration.*

Stuffed Baked Apples with Raisins and Walnuts

Yield: 4 servings | **Prep time:** 15 minutes | **Cook time:** 30 minutes

Ingredients:

- 4 large apples, cored
- 1/2 cup raisins
- 1/2 cup chopped walnuts
- 1/4 cup brown sugar
- 1 teaspoon ground cinnamon
- 1/4 teaspoon ground nutmeg
- 1/2 cup apple juice
- 2 tablespoons butter, cut into small pieces

Directions:

1. Preheat your oven to 350°F (175°C).

2. In a medium bowl, combine the raisins, chopped walnuts, brown sugar, ground cinnamon, and ground nutmeg.

3. Stuff each cored apple with the raisin and walnut mixture.

4. Place the stuffed apples in a baking dish and pour the apple juice around the apples.

5. Dot the tops of the apples with small pieces of butter.

6. Bake in the preheated oven for 30 minutes or until the apples are tender.

7. Let the apples cool slightly before serving.

Nutritional Information: 250 calories, 2g protein, 40g carbohydrates, 10g fat, 5g fiber, 0mg cholesterol, 5mg sodium, 200mg potassium.

Note: *Nutritional values are estimated based on the ingredients and serving size. Actual values may vary slightly. The final presentation of your recipe may vary slightly from the image illustration.*

Almond and Date Energy Balls

Yield: 6 servings | **Prep time:** 15 minutes | **Cook time:** 0 minutes

Ingredients:
- 1 cup pitted dates
- 1 cup raw almonds
- 1/4 cup almond butter
- 2 tablespoons chia seeds
- 1 tablespoon honey
- 1 teaspoon vanilla extract
- 1/4 teaspoon sea salt

Directions:
1. In a food processor, blend the dates and almonds until finely chopped.
2. Add almond butter, chia seeds, honey, vanilla extract, and sea salt. Blend until the mixture forms a sticky dough.
3. Scoop out small portions of the mixture and roll into 1-inch balls.
4. Place the energy balls on a baking sheet lined with parchment paper.
5. Refrigerate for at least 30 minutes to firm up.
6. Store in an airtight container in the refrigerator for up to 1 week.

Nutritional Information: 180 calories, 4g protein, 24g carbohydrates, 9g fat, 4g fiber, 0mg cholesterol, 40mg sodium, 200mg potassium.

Note: *Nutritional values are estimated based on the ingredients and serving size. Actual values may vary slightly. The final presentation of your recipe may vary slightly from the image illustration.*

Pistachio and Honey Baklava

Yield: 6 servings | **Prep time:** 20 minutes | **Cook time:** 40 minutes

Ingredients:
- 1 cup pistachios, finely chopped
- 1/2 cup unsalted butter, melted
- 1/2 cup honey
- 1 teaspoon ground cinnamon
- 1/4 teaspoon ground cloves
- 1 package phyllo dough (16 oz), thawed

Directions:
1. Preheat the oven to 350°F (175°C). Grease a 9x13 inch baking dish.
2. In a bowl, combine the chopped pistachios, ground cinnamon, and ground cloves.
3. Layer 8 sheets of phyllo dough in the baking dish, brushing each sheet with melted butter.
4. Sprinkle a thin layer of the pistachio mixture over the phyllo dough.
5. Repeat the layers of phyllo dough and pistachio mixture until all the pistachio mixture is used, finishing with 8 layers of phyllo dough on top.
6. Cut the baklava into diamond shapes using a sharp knife.
7. Bake in the preheated oven for 40 minutes, or until golden brown and crisp.
8. Drizzle honey over the hot baklava and let it soak in as it cools.

Nutritional Information: 360 calories, 5g protein, 38g carbohydrates, 23g fat, 2g fiber, 20mg cholesterol, 160mg sodium, 200mg potassium.

Note: *Nutritional values are estimated based on the ingredients and serving size. Actual values may vary slightly. The final presentation of your recipe may vary slightly from the image illustration.*

Walnut and Fig Bars	**Peanut Butter and Chia Seed Cookies**

Walnut and Fig Bars

Yield: 6 servings | **Prep time:** 15 minutes | **Cook time:** 25 minutes

Ingredients:
- 1 cup dried figs, chopped
- 1/2 cup walnuts, chopped
- 1/2 cup rolled oats
- 1/2 cup whole wheat flour
- 1/4 cup honey
- 1/4 cup unsalted butter, melted
- 1/2 teaspoon ground cinnamon
- 1/4 teaspoon salt
- 1 teaspoon vanilla extract

Directions:
1. Preheat the oven to 350°F (175°C). Grease an 8x8 inch baking pan.
2. In a large bowl, combine the chopped figs, walnuts, rolled oats, and whole wheat flour.
3. In a separate bowl, mix the honey, melted butter, ground cinnamon, salt, and vanilla extract until well combined.
4. Pour the wet ingredients into the dry ingredients and mix until thoroughly combined.
5. Press the mixture evenly into the prepared baking pan.
6. Bake in the preheated oven for 25 minutes, or until the edges are golden brown.
7. Allow to cool completely before cutting into bars.

Nutritional Information: 240 calories, 4g protein, 34g carbohydrates, 10g fat, 4g fiber, 15mg cholesterol, 60mg sodium, 180mg potassium.

Note: *Nutritional values are estimated based on the ingredients and serving size. Actual values may vary slightly. The final presentation of your recipe may vary slightly from the image illustration.*

Peanut Butter and Chia Seed Cookies

Yield: 6 servings | **Prep time:** 15 minutes | **Cook time:** 10 minutes

Ingredients:
- 1 cup creamy peanut butter
- 1/2 cup granulated sugar
- 1/2 cup packed brown sugar
- 1 large egg
- 1 teaspoon vanilla extract
- 1 teaspoon baking soda
- 2 tablespoons chia seeds
- 1/2 cup rolled oats

Directions:
1. Preheat the oven to 350°F (175°C) and line a baking sheet with parchment paper.
2. In a large bowl, mix the peanut butter, granulated sugar, brown sugar, egg, and vanilla extract until well combined.
3. Stir in the baking soda, chia seeds, and rolled oats until evenly distributed.
4. Scoop tablespoon-sized portions of the dough onto the prepared baking sheet, flattening each slightly with a fork.
5. Bake for 10 minutes, or until the edges are golden brown.
6. Allow the cookies to cool on the baking sheet for 5 minutes before transferring to a wire rack to cool completely.

Nutritional Information: 250 calories, 7g protein, 22g carbohydrates, 16g fat, 3g fiber, 15mg cholesterol, 120mg sodium, 200mg potassium.

Note: *Nutritional values are estimated based on the ingredients and serving size. Actual values may vary slightly. The final presentation of your recipe may vary slightly from the image illustration.*

Carrot and Ginger Juice

Yield: 4 servings | **Prep time:** 10 minutes | **Cook time:** 0 minutes

Ingredients:
- 1 lb carrots, peeled and chopped
- 1-inch piece of fresh ginger, peeled and sliced
- 1 cup water
- 1 tablespoon lemon juice (optional)

Directions:
1. Add the chopped carrots, ginger, and water to a blender.
2. Blend until smooth.
3. Strain the mixture through a fine mesh sieve or cheesecloth into a pitcher.
4. Stir in the lemon juice if using.
5. Pour into glasses and serve immediately.

Nutritional Information: 50 calories, 1g protein, 12g carbohydrates, 0g fat, 2g fiber, 0mg cholesterol, 40mg sodium, 250mg potassium.

Note: *Nutritional values are estimated based on the ingredients and serving size. Actual values may vary slightly. The final presentation of your recipe may vary slightly from the image illustration.*

Beet and Apple Juice

Yield: 4 servings | **Prep time:** 10 minutes | **Cook time:** 0 minutes

Ingredients:
- 2 medium beets, peeled and chopped
- 2 large apples, cored and chopped
- 1 cup water
- 1 tablespoon lemon juice (optional)

Directions:
1. Add the chopped beets, apples, and water to a blender.
2. Blend until smooth.
3. Strain the mixture through a fine mesh sieve or cheesecloth into a pitcher.
4. Stir in the lemon juice if using.
5. Pour into glasses and serve immediately.

Nutritional Information: 60 calories, 1g protein, 14g carbohydrates, 0g fat, 2g fiber, 0mg cholesterol, 35mg sodium, 300mg potassium.

Note: *Nutritional values are estimated based on the ingredients and serving size. Actual values may vary slightly. The final presentation of your recipe may vary slightly from the image illustration.*

Citrus Blast Juice (Orange, Grapefruit, and Lemon)

Yield: 4 servings | **Prep time:** 10 minutes | **Cook time:** 0 minutes

Ingredients:

- 4 oranges, peeled and segmented
- 2 grapefruits, peeled and segmented
- 2 lemons, juiced
- 1 tablespoon honey (optional)
- 1 cup water

Directions:

1. Add the oranges, grapefruits, lemon juice, and water to a blender.

2. Blend until smooth.

3. Strain the mixture through a fine mesh sieve or cheesecloth into a pitcher.

4. Stir in honey, if using.

5. Pour into glasses and serve immediately.

Nutritional Information: 80 calories, 1g protein, 20g carbohydrates, 0g fat, 3g fiber, 0mg cholesterol, 0mg sodium, 350mg potassium.

Note: *Nutritional values are estimated based on the ingredients and serving size. Actual values may vary slightly. The final presentation of your recipe may vary slightly from the image illustration.*

Pineapple and Mango Juice

Yield: 4 servings | **Prep time:** 10 minutes | **Cook time:** 0 minutes

Ingredients:

- 2 cups fresh pineapple chunks
- 2 cups fresh mango chunks
- 1 cup water
- 1 tablespoon lime juice (optional)
- 1 tablespoon honey (optional)

Directions:

1. Add the pineapple chunks, mango chunks, and water to a blender.

2. Blend until smooth.

3. Strain the mixture through a fine mesh sieve or cheesecloth into a pitcher.

4. Stir in lime juice and honey, if using.

5. Pour into glasses and serve immediately.

Nutritional Information: 110 calories, 1g protein, 28g carbohydrates, 0g fat, 2g fiber, 0mg cholesterol, 2mg sodium, 300mg potassium.

Note: *Nutritional values are estimated based on the ingredients and serving size. Actual values may vary slightly. The final presentation of your recipe may vary slightly from the image illustration.*

Chamomile and Lavender Tea

Yield: 4 servings | **Prep time:** 5 minutes | **Cook time:** 10 minutes

Ingredients:
- 4 cups water
- 2 tablespoons dried chamomile flowers
- 1 tablespoon dried lavender flowers
- 1 tablespoon honey (optional)
- Lemon slices for garnish (optional)

Directions:
1. In a medium saucepan, bring 4 cups of water to a boil.
2. Remove from heat and add the dried chamomile and lavender flowers to the hot water.
3. Cover the saucepan and let the tea steep for 5-7 minutes.
4. Strain the tea into a teapot or directly into serving cups.
5. Add honey to sweeten, if desired.
6. Garnish with lemon slices if desired.
7. Serve hot and enjoy.

Nutritional Information: 5 calories, 0g protein, 1g carbohydrates, 0g fat, 0g fiber, 0mg cholesterol, 5mg sodium, 10mg potassium.

Note: *Nutritional values are estimated based on the ingredients and serving size. Actual values may vary slightly. The final presentation of your recipe may vary slightly from the image illustration.*

Mint and Ginger Tea

Yield: 4 servings | **Prep time:** 5 minutes | **Cook time:** 10 minutes

Ingredients:
- 4 cups water
- 1/4 cup fresh mint leaves
- 1-inch piece of fresh ginger, sliced
- 1 tablespoon honey (optional)
- Lemon slices for garnish (optional)

Directions:
1. In a medium saucepan, bring 4 cups of water to a boil.
2. Add the fresh mint leaves and ginger slices to the boiling water.
3. Reduce heat and let the mixture simmer for 5 minutes.
4. Remove from heat and let the tea steep for an additional 5 minutes.
5. Strain the tea into a teapot or directly into serving cups.
6. Add honey to sweeten, if desired.
7. Garnish with lemon slices if desired.
8. Serve hot and enjoy.

Nutritional Information: 10 calories, 0g protein, 2g carbohydrates, 0g fat, 0g fiber, 0mg cholesterol, 5mg sodium, 10mg potassium.

Note: *Nutritional values are estimated based on the ingredients and serving size. Actual values may vary slightly. The final presentation of your recipe may vary slightly from the image illustration.*

Lemon Balm and Honey Tea

Yield: 2 to 6 servings | **Prep time:** 5 minutes | **Cook time:** 10 minutes

Ingredients:
- 4 cups water
- 1/4 cup fresh lemon balm leaves (or 2 tablespoons dried lemon balm)
- 2 tablespoons honey
- 1 lemon, sliced

Directions:
1. In a medium pot, bring 4 cups of water to a boil.
2. Add the lemon balm leaves and reduce the heat. Let it simmer for 5 minutes.
3. Remove the pot from the heat and let the tea steep for another 5 minutes.
4. Strain the tea into cups.
5. Add honey to each cup and stir until dissolved.
6. Garnish with a slice of lemon.

Nutritional Information: 60 calories, 0g protein, 17g carbohydrates, 0g fat, 0g fiber, 0mg cholesterol, 5mg sodium, 60mg potassium.

Note: *Nutritional values are estimated based on the ingredients and serving size. Actual values may vary slightly. The final presentation of your recipe may vary slightly from the image illustration.*

Hibiscus and Rosehip Tea

Yield: 4 servings | **Prep time:** 5 minutes | **Cook time:** 10 minutes

Ingredients:
- 4 cups water
- 2 tablespoons dried hibiscus flowers
- 2 tablespoons dried rosehips
- 1-2 tablespoons honey (optional)
- Lemon slices for garnish (optional)

Directions:
1. In a medium saucepan, bring 4 cups of water to a boil.
2. Add the dried hibiscus flowers and dried rosehips to the boiling water.
3. Reduce heat and let the mixture simmer for 5 minutes.
4. Remove from heat and let the tea steep for an additional 5 minutes.
5. Strain the tea into a teapot or directly into serving cups.
6. Add honey to sweeten, if desired.
7. Garnish with lemon slices if desired.
8. Serve hot and enjoy.

Nutritional Information: 70 calories, 0g protein, 18g carbohydrates, 0g fat, 0g fiber, 0mg cholesterol, 5mg sodium, 50mg potassium.

Note: *Nutritional values are estimated based on the ingredients and serving size. Actual values may vary slightly. The final presentation of your recipe may vary slightly from the image illustration.*

Cucumber, Lemon, and Mint Water

Yield: 4 servings | **Prep time:** 10 minutes | **Cook time:** 0 minutes

Ingredients:
- 4 cups water
- 1/2 cucumber, thinly sliced
- 1 lemon, thinly sliced
- 1/4 cup fresh mint leaves
- Ice cubes (optional)

Directions:
1. In a large pitcher, add the water.
2. Add the sliced cucumber, lemon, and mint leaves to the pitcher.
3. Stir the ingredients gently to combine.
4. Let the mixture sit for at least 10 minutes to allow the flavors to infuse.
5. Add ice cubes if desired.
6. Serve chilled and enjoy.

Nutritional Information: 5 calories, 0g protein, 1g carbohydrates, 0g fat, 0g fiber, 0mg cholesterol, 5mg sodium, 10mg potassium.

Note: *Nutritional values are estimated based on the ingredients and serving size. Actual values may vary slightly. The final presentation of your recipe may vary slightly from the image illustration.*

Orange and Blueberry Water

Yield: 4 servings | **Prep time:** 10 minutes | **Cook time:** 0 minutes

Ingredients:
- 4 cups water
- 1 orange, thinly sliced
- 1/2 cup fresh blueberries
- Ice cubes (optional)

Directions:
1. In a large pitcher, add the water.
2. Add the orange slices and fresh blueberries to the pitcher.
3. Stir gently to combine the ingredients.
4. Let the mixture sit for at least 10 minutes to allow the flavors to infuse.
5. Add ice cubes if desired.
6. Serve chilled and enjoy.

Nutritional Information: 15 calories, 0g protein, 4g carbohydrates, 0g fat, 0g fiber, 0mg cholesterol, 5mg sodium, 25mg potassium.

Note: *Nutritional values are estimated based on the ingredients and serving size. Actual values may vary slightly. The final presentation of your recipe may vary slightly from the image illustration.*

Watermelon and Lime Water

Yield: 4 servings | **Prep time:** 10 minutes | **Cook time:** 0 minutes

Ingredients:
- 4 cups water
- 2 cups watermelon, cubed
- 1 lime, thinly sliced
- Ice cubes (optional)

Directions:
1. In a large pitcher, add the water.
2. Add the cubed watermelon and lime slices to the pitcher.
3. Stir gently to combine the ingredients.
4. Let the mixture sit for at least 10 minutes to allow the flavors to infuse.
5. Add ice cubes if desired.
6. Serve chilled and enjoy.

Nutritional Information: 20 calories, 0g protein, 5g carbohydrates, 0g fat, 0g fiber, 0mg cholesterol, 5mg sodium, 30mg potassium.

Note: *Nutritional values are estimated based on the ingredients and serving size. Actual values may vary slightly. The final presentation of your recipe may vary slightly from the image illustration.*

Pineapple and Coconut Water

Yield: 4 servings | **Prep time:** 10 minutes | **Cook time:** 0 minutes

Ingredients:
- 4 cups coconut water
- 1 cup pineapple chunks
- Ice cubes (optional)

Directions:
1. In a large pitcher, add the coconut water.
2. Add the pineapple chunks to the pitcher.
3. Stir gently to combine the ingredients.
4. Let the mixture sit for at least 10 minutes to allow the flavors to infuse.
5. Add ice cubes if desired.
6. Serve chilled and enjoy.

Nutritional Information: 40 calories, 0g protein, 10g carbohydrates, 0g fat, 1g fiber, 0mg cholesterol, 20mg sodium, 150mg potassium.

Note: *Nutritional values are estimated based on the ingredients and serving size. Actual values may vary slightly. The final presentation of your recipe may vary slightly from the image illustration.*

If you find yourself missing ingredients for a specific dish from the meal plan, substitute it with another recipe from the book that matches calories and the appropriate meal time. Additionally, if you have severe health conditions, it's essential to consult with your healthcare provider before starting the 35-day meal plan to ensure it suits your health needs.

MONDAY			
Breakfast	**Lunch**	**Dinner**	**Snacks**
Tropical Fruit and Coconut Yogurt Parfait (320 calories, 10 min prep and cooking time) – **Page 11**	Couscous Salad with Chickpeas and Lemon (220 calories, 20 min prep and cooking time) – **Page 33**	Grilled Salmon with Lemon and Dill (350 calories, 25 min prep and cooking time) – **Page 56**	Date and Nut Energy Bars (210 calories, 15 min prep and cooking time) – **Page 23**

TUESDAY			
Breakfast	**Lunch**	**Dinner**	**Snacks**
Avocado Toast with Cherry Tomatoes and Basil (300 calories, 10 min prep and cooking time) – **Page 15**	Classic Greek Salad (180 calories, 15 min prep and cooking time) – **Page 35**	Baked Cod with Tomatoes and Olives (220 calories, 30 min prep and cooking time) – **Page 56**	Crispy Baked Zucchini Fries (180 calories, 35 min prep and cooking time) – **Page 29**

WEDNESDAY			
Breakfast	**Lunch**	**Dinner**	**Snacks**
Creamy Millet Porridge with Dried Fruits (350 calories, 30 min prep and cooking time) – **Page 18**	Falafel Wrap with Tzatziki (350 calories, 35 min prep and cooking time) – **Page 50**	Spaghetti with Pesto and Cherry Tomatoes (400 calories, 25 min prep and cooking time) – **Page 62**	Classic Hummus (140 calories, 10 min prep and cooking time) – **Page 21**

THURSDAY			
Breakfast	**Lunch**	**Dinner**	**Snacks**
Greek Yogurt with Honey and Mixed Nuts (260 calories, 5 min prep and cooking time) – **Page 12**	Grilled Zucchini and Bell Pepper Salad (180 calories, 25 min prep and cooking time) – **Page 37**	Chicken Souvlaki with Tzatziki (380 calories, 35 min prep and cooking time) – **Page 46**	Tzatziki (Cucumber Yogurt Dip) (60 calories, 10 min prep and cooking time) – **Page 21**

FRIDAY			
Breakfast	**Lunch**	**Dinner**	**Snacks**
Berry Banana Smoothie with Greek Yogurt (220 calories, 5 min prep and cooking time) – **Page 19**	Quinoa Bowl with Roasted Vegetables and Feta (290 calories, 45 min prep and cooking time) – **Page 43**	Grilled Salmon with Lemon and Dill (350 calories, 25 min prep and cooking time) – **Page 56**	Baba Ganoush (Roasted Eggplant Dip) (110 calories, 50 min prep and cooking time) – **Page 22**

SATURDAY			
Breakfast	**Lunch**	**Dinner**	**Snacks**
Spinach and Mushroom Frittata (220 calories, 30 min prep and cooking time) – **Page 13**	Brown Rice Bowl with Grilled Chicken and Avocado (450 calories, 45 min prep and cooking time) – **Page 43**	Grilled Salmon with Lemon and Dill (350 calories, 25 min prep and cooking time) – **Page 56**	Tzatziki (Cucumber Yogurt Dip) (60 calories, 10 min prep and cooking time) – **Page 21**

SUNDAY			
Breakfast	**Lunch**	**Dinner**	**Snacks**
Warm Cinnamon Apple Oatmeal (320 calories, 15 min prep and cooking time) – **Page 18**	Calamari Salad with Olives and Capers (220 calories, 25 min prep and cooking time) – **Page 41**	Stuffed Zucchini Boats with Lentils and Rice (210 calories, 55 min prep and cooking time) – **Page 65**	Marinated Artichoke Hearts (110 calories, 10 min prep and cooking time) – **Page 30**

MONDAY

Breakfast	Lunch	Dinner	Snacks
Berry and Granola Parfait (350 calories, 10 min prep and cooking time) – **Page 12**	Roasted Beet and Goat Cheese Salad (250 calories, 55 min prep and cooking time) – **Page 38**	Lamb Chops with Rosemary and Garlic (400 calories, 25 min prep and cooking time) – **Page 59**	Carrot and Cucumber Sticks with Tahini Dip (160 calories, 15 min prep and cooking time) – **Page 30**

TUESDAY

Breakfast	Lunch	Dinner	Snacks
Greek Yogurt with Honey and Mixed Nuts (260 calories, 5 min prep and cooking time) – **Page 12**	Brown Rice Bowl with Grilled Chicken and Avocado (450 calories, 45 min prep and cooking time) – **Page 43**	Risotto with Asparagus and Parmesan (350 calories, 40 min prep and cooking time) – **Page 62**	Classic Hummus (140 calories, 10 min prep and cooking time) – **Page 21**

WEDNESDAY

Breakfast	Lunch	Dinner	Snacks
Grilled Cheese with Spinach and Feta (450 calories, 15 min prep and cooking time) – **Page 16**	Shrimp and Avocado Salad (350 calories, 25 min prep and cooking time) – **Page 40**	Paella with Chicken and Seafood (550 calories, 55 min prep and cooking time) – **Page 64**	Rosemary Cashews (210 calories, 20 min prep and cooking time) – **Page 28**

THURSDAY

Breakfast	Lunch	Dinner	Snacks
Avocado Toast with Cherry Tomatoes and Basil (300 calories, 10 min prep and cooking time) – **Page 15**	Butternut Squash and Chickpea Stew (250 calories, 60 min prep and cooking time) – **Page 66**	Baked Cod with Tomatoes and Olives (220 calories, 30 min prep and cooking time) – **Page 56**	Classic Hummus (140 calories, 10 min prep and cooking time) – **Page 21**

FRIDAY

Breakfast	Lunch	Dinner	Snacks
Tomato and Olive Tapenade Bruschetta (180 calories, 15 min prep and cooking time) – **Page 16**	Mediterranean Quinoa Salad (250 calories, 30 min prep and cooking time) – **Page 33**	Chicken Marsala with Mushrooms (400 calories, 30 min prep and cooking time) – **Page 59**	Marinated Artichoke Hearts (110 calories, 10 min prep and cooking time) – **Page 30**

SATURDAY

Breakfast	Lunch	Dinner	Snacks
Quinoa Breakfast Bowl with Nuts and Fruits (350 calories, 25 min prep and cooking time) – **Page 17**	Chicken Souvlaki with Tzatziki (380 calories, 35 min prep and cooking time) – **Page 46**	Grilled Salmon with Lemon and Dill (350 calories, 25 min prep and cooking time) – **Page 56**	Spiced Roasted Almonds (200 calories, 20 min prep and cooking time) – **Page 27**

SUNDAY

Breakfast	Lunch	Dinner	Snacks
Overnight Oats with Berries and Honey (290 calories, 5 min prep and cooking time) – **Page 17**	Mediterranean Veggie Pita (300 calories, 15 min prep and cooking time) – **Page 49**	Pork Tenderloin with Apple Cider Glaze (300 calories, 45 min prep and cooking time) – **Page 60**	Grapes and Goat Cheese Platter (180 calories, 10 min prep and cooking time) – **Page 25**

MONDAY

Breakfast	Lunch	Dinner	Snacks
Creamy Millet Porridge with Dried Fruits (350 calories, 30 min prep and cooking time) – **Page 18**	Grilled Chicken and Hummus Wrap (400 calories, 30 min prep and cooking time) – **Page 49**	Seared Scallops with Lemon Butter Sauce (320 calories, 20 min prep and cooking time) – **Page 57**	Tzatziki (Cucumber Yogurt Dip) (60 calories, 10 min prep and cooking time) – **Page 21**

TUESDAY

Breakfast	Lunch	Dinner	Snacks
Spinach and Mushroom Frittata (220 calories, 30 min prep and cooking time) – **Page 13**	Brown Rice Bowl with Grilled Chicken and Avocado (450 calories, 45 min prep and cooking time) – **Page 43**	Vegetable Paella (320 calories, 60 min prep and cooking time) – **Page 65**	Fig and Brie Bites (150 calories, 10 min prep and cooking time) – **Page 25**

WEDNESDAY

Breakfast	Lunch	Dinner	Snacks
Mango and Turmeric Smoothie (220 calories, 5 min prep and cooking time) – **Page 20**	Quinoa Bowl with Roasted Vegetables and Feta (290 calories, 45 min prep and cooking time) – **Page 43**	Beef Stroganoff with Sour Cream and Dill (450 calories, 45 min prep and cooking time) – **Page 60**	Sesame Seed Brittle (210 calories, 25 min prep and cooking time) – **Page 28**

THURSDAY

Breakfast	Lunch	Dinner	Snacks
Greek Yogurt with Honey and Mixed Nuts (260 calories, 5 min prep and cooking time) – **Page 12**	Lentil Soup with Spinach and Lemon (220 calories, 45 min prep and cooking time) – **Page 51**	Mussels in White Wine Sauce (220 calories, 30 min prep and cooking time) – **Page 58**	Coconut and Almond Energy Balls (180 calories, 15 min prep and cooking time) – **Page 24**

FRIDAY

Breakfast	Lunch	Dinner	Snacks
Scrambled Eggs with Smoked Salmon (240 calories, 10 min prep and cooking time) – **Page 14**	Shrimp and Avocado Salad (350 calories, 25 min prep and cooking time) – **Page 40**	Butternut Squash and Chickpea Stew (250 calories, 60 min prep and cooking time) – **Page 66**	Pear and Blue Cheese Salad (220 calories, 10 min prep and cooking time) – **Page 26**

SATURDAY

Breakfast	Lunch	Dinner	Snacks
Avocado Toast with Cherry Tomatoes and Basil (300 calories, 10 min prep and cooking time) – **Page 15**	Couscous Bowl with Chickpeas and Mint (280 calories, 20 min prep and cooking time) – **Page 44**	Baked Cod with Tomatoes and Olives (220 calories, 30 min prep and cooking time) – **Page 56**	Honey-Glazed Walnuts (250 calories, 15 min prep and cooking time) – **Page 27**

SUNDAY

Breakfast	Lunch	Dinner	Snacks
Warm Cinnamon Apple Oatmeal (320 calories, 15 min prep and cooking time) – **Page 18**	Spinach and Strawberry Salad with Balsamic Vinaigrette (180 calories, 10 min prep and cooking time) – **Page 35**	Chicken Marsala with Mushrooms (400 calories, 30 min prep and cooking time) – **Page 59**	Spiced Roasted Almonds (200 calories, 20 min prep and cooking time) – **Page 27**

MONDAY

Breakfast	Lunch	Dinner	Snacks
Tropical Fruit and Coconut Yogurt Parfait (320 calories, 10 min prep and cooking time) – Page 11	Mediterranean Quinoa Salad (250 calories, 30 min prep and cooking time) – Page 33	Grilled Steak with Chimichurri Sauce (350 calories, 25 min prep and cooking time) – Page 61	Roasted Chickpeas with Paprika (150 calories, 30 min prep and cooking time) – Page 29

TUESDAY

Breakfast	Lunch	Dinner	Snacks
Shakshuka (Poached Eggs in Tomato Sauce) (180 calories, 30 min prep and cooking time) – Page 13	Falafel Wrap with Tzatziki (350 calories, 35 min prep and cooking time) – Page 50	Fish Stew with Saffron and Potatoes (320 calories, 45 min prep and cooking time) – Page 57	Red Pepper and Walnut Muhammar (180 calories, 10 min prep and cooking time) – Page 22

WEDNESDAY

Breakfast	Lunch	Dinner	Snacks
Berry Banana Smoothie with Greek Yogurt (220 calories, 5 min prep and cooking time) – Page 19	Brown Rice and Black Bean Salad (250 calories, 45 min prep and cooking time) – Page 34	Lamb Chops with Rosemary and Garlic (400 calories, 25 min prep and cooking time) – Page 59	Rosemary Cashews (210 calories, 20 min prep and cooking time) – Page 28

THURSDAY

Breakfast	Lunch	Dinner	Snacks
Mediterranean Breakfast Wrap with Eggs and Veggies (350 calories, 20 min prep and cooking time) – Page 14	Vegetable Minestrone (200 calories, 50 min prep and cooking time) – Page 52	Grilled Salmon with Lemon and Dill (350 calories, 25 min prep and cooking time) – Page 56	Melon and Prosciutto Skewers (150 calories, 10 min prep and cooking time) – Page 26

FRIDAY

Breakfast	Lunch	Dinner	Snacks
Peach and Ginger Smoothie (180 calories, 5 min prep and cooking time) – Page 20	Barley Bowl with Mushrooms and Spinach (320 calories, 45 min prep and cooking time) – Page 44	Eggplant Parmesan (400 calories, 70 min prep and cooking time) – Page 54	Carrot and Cucumber Sticks with Tahini Dip (160 calories, 15 min prep and cooking time) – Page 30

SATURDAY

Breakfast	Lunch	Dinner	Snacks
Greek Yogurt with Honey and Mixed Nuts (260 calories, 5 min prep and cooking time) – Page 12	Watercress Salad with Feta and Olives (180 calories, 10 min prep and cooking time) – Page 36	Spaghetti with Pesto and Cherry Tomatoes (400 calories, 25 min prep and cooking time) – Page 62	Fig and Brie Bites (150 calories, 10 min prep and cooking time) – Page 25

SUNDAY

Breakfast	Lunch	Dinner	Snacks
Creamy Millet Porridge with Dried Fruits (350 calories, 30 min prep and cooking time) – Page 18	Turkey Meatballs with Zucchini Noodles (310 calories, 45 min prep and cooking time) – Page 48	Tuna Steaks with Avocado Salsa (320 calories, 25 min prep and cooking time) – Page 58	Pear and Blue Cheese Salad (220 calories, 10 min prep and cooking time) – Page 26

MONDAY

Breakfast	Lunch	Dinner	Snacks
Spinach and Mushroom Frittata (220 calories, 30 min prep and cooking time) – **Page 13**	Lentil Soup with Spinach and Lemon (220 calories, 45 min prep and cooking time) – **Page 51**	Seared Scallops with Lemon Butter Sauce (320 calories, 20 min prep and cooking time) – Page 57	Classic Hummus (140 calories, 10 min prep and cooking time) – Page 21

TUESDAY

Breakfast	Lunch	Dinner	Snacks
Greek Yogurt with Honey and Mixed Nuts (260 calories, 5 min prep and cooking time) – Page 12	Roasted Vegetable Salad with Balsamic Glaze (200 calories, 40 min prep and cooking time) – **Page 37**	Stuffed Peppers with Ground Turkey and Quinoa (340 calories, 60 min prep and cooking time) – Page 47	Red Pepper and Walnut Muhammar (180 calories, 10 min prep and cooking time) – Page 22

WEDNESDAY

Breakfast	Lunch	Dinner	Snacks
Warm Cinnamon Apple Oatmeal (320 calories, 15 min prep and cooking time) – **Page 18**	Chickpea Salad with Cucumber and Mint (220 calories, 15 min prep and cooking time) – **Page 31**	Lamb Chops with Rosemary and Garlic (400 calories, 25 min prep and cooking time) – Page 59	Spiced Roasted Almonds (200 calories, 20 min prep and cooking time) – **Page 27**

THURSDAY

Breakfast	Lunch	Dinner	Snacks
Berry and Granola Parfait (350 calories, 10 min prep and cooking time) – **Page 12**	Roasted Beet and Goat Cheese Salad (250 calories, 55 min prep and cooking time) – Page 38	Paella with Chicken and Seafood (550 calories, 55 min prep and cooking time) – Page 64	Marinated Artichoke Hearts (110 calories, 10 min prep and cooking time) – **Page 30**

FRIDAY

Breakfast	Lunch	Dinner	Snacks
Avocado Toast with Cherry Tomatoes and Basil (300 calories, 10 min prep and cooking time) – **Page 15**	Lentil Soup with Spinach and Lemon (220 calories, 45 min prep and cooking time) – **Page 51**	Baked Ziti with Sausage and Peppers (550 calories, 60 min prep and cooking time) – Page 64	Spiced Roasted Almonds (200 calories, 20 min prep and cooking time) – **Page 27**

SATURDAY

Breakfast	Lunch	Dinner	Snacks
Greek Yogurt with Honey and Mixed Nuts (260 calories, 5 min prep and cooking time) – Page 12	Watercress Salad with Feta and Olives (180 calories, 10 min prep and cooking time) – Page 36	Spaghetti with Pesto and Cherry Tomatoes (400 calories, 25 min prep and cooking time) – Page 62	Fig and Brie Bites (150 calories, 10 min prep and cooking time) – Page 25

SUNDAY

Breakfast	Lunch	Dinner	Snacks
Creamy Millet Porridge with Dried Fruits (350 calories, 30 min prep and cooking time) – Page 18	Chicken and Orzo Soup (250 calories, 40 min prep and cooking time) – Page 52	Tuna Steaks with Avocado Salsa (320 calories, 25 min prep and cooking time) – Page 58	Pear and Blue Cheese Salad (220 calories, 10 min prep and cooking time) – Page 26

BONUS EBOOK: 50 ADDITIONAL MEDITERRANEAN RECIPES

We're excited to offer you a special bonus by purchasing this Mediterranean Diet Cookbook—a complimentary eBook filled with 50 more Mediterranean recipes! This exclusive collection is designed to expand your culinary horizons and bring even more delicious and healthy dishes into your kitchen.

What's Inside?

This bonus eBook is organized into five chapters, each brimming with recipes that showcase the vibrant flavors and wholesome ingredients of the Mediterranean region:

Chapter 1: Salads
Explore fresh and vibrant salads, including bean and legume salads, grain salads, and leafy green salads. Perfect as a side dish or a light meal, these salads are bursting with nutrition and taste.

Chapter 2: Lunches
Discover a variety of satisfying pasta dishes and sandwiches perfect for a hearty lunch. From classic Italian favorites to innovative wraps, these recipes are easy to prepare and flavorful.

Chapter 3: Dinners
Delight in comforting casseroles and bakes, savory meat dishes, and creative vegetable main courses. These dinners are designed to be both nourishing and delicious, ensuring you can enjoy a fulfilling Mediterranean meal any night of the week.

Chapter 4: Desserts
Indulge in sweet treats that are as healthy as they are delicious. From Greek yogurt popsicles to decadent chocolate ruffles, these desserts will satisfy your sweet tooth without compromising your commitment to the Mediterranean diet.

Chapter 5: Drinks
Quench your thirst with a selection of refreshing juices, smoothies, light alcoholic beverages, and specialty drinks. These drinks are perfect for any occasion, whether starting your day with a detox juice or unwinding with a Limoncello Sparkler.

HOW TO ACCESS?

Simply scan the QR code below with your smartphone or tablet, and you'll be directed to download your free E-book instantly.

or follow the link https://www.olivermaxwellbooks.com/bonus-50-mediterranean-recipes-ebook

We hope this bonus eBook inspires you to continue exploring the rich culinary traditions of the Mediterranean. With these dditional recipes, you'll have even more options to enjoy this celebrated diet's flavors and health benefits.

Thank You

Gratitude for Embracing the Mediterranean Lifestyle!

As you reach the final pages of "The True Mediterranean Diet Cookbook for Beginners," I want to express my sincere appreciation for choosing this book as your guide on this flavorful and healthful journey. Your commitment to adopting a Mediterranean lifestyle is truly inspiring, and I am honored to have been a part of your culinary adventure.

Cooking is a joyful experience that goes beyond the ingredients; it's a way to nourish your body, uplift your spirit, and connect with the rich traditions of the Mediterranean. Each recipe in this book was designed to bring the essence of the Mediterranean to your kitchen, offering both delicious meals and a path to better health.

Your Feedback Matters!

I would love to hear about your journey with the recipes in this book. Your feedback is invaluable and helps shape future projects. Whether you found new favorites, made your own adaptations, or simply enjoyed the process, please share your experiences!

Thank you for placing your trust in this book. May your kitchen always be filled with the vibrant flavors of the Mediterranean, your meals with warmth, and your life with lasting health and happiness.

Happy Cooking

Oliver Maxwe

Made in United States
Orlando, FL
15 October 2024